T0322380

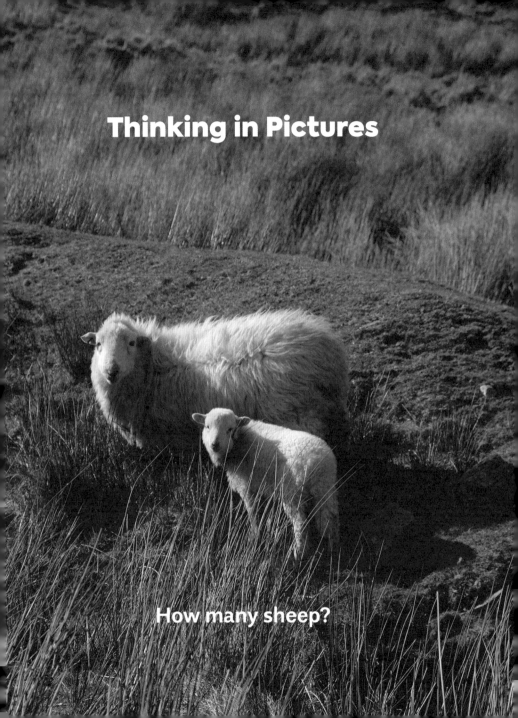

Also by Michael Blastland

The Hidden Half: How the World Conceals its Secrets

The Norm Chronicles:
Stories and Numbers About Danger (with David Spiegelhalter)

The Tiger That Isn't:
Seeing the World Through Numbers (with Andrew Dilnot)

Joe: The Only Boy in the World

Thinking in Pictures

Adventures in Trying to be Smart

Michael Blastland

Atlantic Books
London

First published in hardback in Great Britain in 2023 by Atlantic Books, an imprint of Atlantic Books Ltd.

10 9 8 7 6 5 4 3 2 1

A CIP catalogue record for this book is available from the British Library.

Hardback ISBN: 978-1-83895-746-9
E-book ISBN: 978-1-83895-747-6

Printed in Great Britain by Bell and Bain Ltd, Glasgow

Atlantic Books
An imprint of Atlantic Books Ltd
Ormond House
26–27 Boswell Street
London
WC1N 3JZ

www.atlantic-books.co.uk

For Kitty, Cait and Katey

If I can't picture it, I can't understand it.

Albert Einstein

Contents

1

Why thinking in pictures?

Short answer: because some people see better that way. They think visually. Maybe you're one of them.

But also for a stranger reason: because the words about thinking seem to need help.

To see what I mean, sample a few of the many hot popscience books to hit the shelves lately which all promise a smarter, more seeing, more rational you. No need to read this list, just imagine the blaze of light:

- *Rationality* by Steven Pinker
- *Calling Bullshit* by Jevon West and Carl Bergstrom
- *How to Make the World Add Up* by Tim Harford
- *How to Read Numbers* by David Chivers and Tom Chivers
- *The End of Bias* by Jessica Nordell
- *How to Decide* by Annie Duke
- *The Great Mental Models, Volume 1* by Rhiannon Beaubien and Shane Parrish
- *Noise* by Daniel Kahneman, Olivier Sibony and Cass Sunstein
- *Anthro-Vision* by Gillian Tett

- *Thinking Better* by Marcus du Sautoy
- *Super Thinking* by Gabriel Weinberg and Lauren McCann
- *Emotional: The New Thinking About Feelings* by Leonard Mlodinow
- *The Skeptics' Guide to the Universe* by Steven Novella
- *How to Think* by Tom Chatfield
- *Think Again* by Adam Grant
- *The Scout Mindset* by Julia Galef
- *The Irrational Ape* by David Grimes

There are more – lots – plus blogs, articles, podcasts, videos and a million tweets.

How this wave of DIY cleverness grew so big, I'm not sure. It seems partly to have begun with psychological research in the 1970s on decision-making that gave new impetus and a sciencey vibe to the ancient and satisfying art of telling other people they were wrong. Then a little over a decade ago, this became a genre with a name – smart-thinking – and now there's no end to it. See deeper, reason better, make sense of numbers, avoid bias and noise, improve decisions, spot fakery... It's all there on the shelves or online, and it can all be yours.[1]

Reading a heap of these books, I thought: 'Hmm, they're good, mostly.' Then, piling them on top of the others I'd racked up over the years: 'So much smartness, so many answers.'

But something about that pile of books has also begun to bug me. So many answers, true, but still a nagging question: do they actually, like... you know... *work*? That's to say, have all these books succeeded in moving the dial of people's reasoning and understanding about the world? Or are they like the promises in glossy magazines: a new, slimmer you, every month?[2]

Not sure how we'd measure trends in the general savvy relative to the volume of advice, but on the one hand here's all this rationality and truth-seeking, sometimes pitched as the one manual you need to rewire your brain, while on the other hand the world still seems angry and puzzled, maybe even at a new peak of stupid according to one smart-thinker who says we've grown more outraged and less reflective.[3] Meanwhile, policy and business blunders seem as prolific as ever, every side says it knows but none can agree, and even science is said to be going through a replication crisis of gross un-smart-ness among some of the smartest, most well-trained thinkers of all.[4] Why, with so much smart-thinking, isn't there more smart-thinking? Why, if the books are that good, are there so many?

Not least, have they helped me? Sure, I've picked up ideas and techniques, but why after years of self-improvement am I still not a decision-making, bias-spotting, rational paragon, dammit? Getting ideas off the page somehow doesn't seem so easy.

So I began casting around for reasons. Maybe the books/blogs, etc., don't work because the ideas are crap; they're a fad, a pile-in, out to make a buck from readers craving the elixir of clever. Or maybe they do work, or work OK-ish, but they're three-quarters hype, or preaching only to that famous small band of the converted. Or are they written by a bunch of relatively rich blokes (mainly) trying to claim reason as their own, passing it off as universal, objective and apolitical when maybe it's no such thing? Or is it precisely because the forces of stupidity are on the rise that we're seeing a smart fight-back?

Maybe the books are vitally distinctive, every one, but this is a long, slow crawl into the light because we're so set in our dumb ways. Maybe it really is like DIY: easy to say, 'I'll just fix that leak' – in practice not so 'just'.

Though truth be told, I was only trying to find fault with the books because I wanted to write another (gotta justify adding to the pile). Smart-thinkers call this 'motivated reasoning', meaning that the way I was assessing the evidence was corrupted by self-interest. Motivated reasoning is bad, they say; you fail to see things as they really are because you're too invested in finding an answer you like. Since no one writing about thinking wants to be accused of bad thoughts, I paused, agonized... then realized I could call it 'constructive criticism' instead, which sounded cool, and carried on, asking, 'What else?' – what are the books missing? Because either they needed a 'What else?' or I did.

Cut to the chase: after long reflection about where the genre was going wrong, I finally concluded...

It wasn't – probably. Not really. It had its faults (one in particular we'll come to), and there's hype and junk out there for sure, but many of the books were good after all, no denying. Maybe this is just a tough gig in an unforgiving world.

Ah well, no harm asking.[5]

This lot, shrunk, plus pics, etc.

Then around this time, one idle afternoon, I came across one of the pictures that eventually found its way into this book – and did a double-take. The picture (of a bicycle chicane on a footpath; you'll see it on page 168) could almost have been designed to illuminate some aspect of smart-thinking out in the wild, or it could if you chose to see it that way and you'd just been reading what I had. 'Huh, it fits!' I thought, in my best Cinderella. 'Picture... thousand words... whaddyaknow!'

And in that moment – pure chance – a vague idea: that maybe the books could say it better if they showed it too, with pictures; a small hope for a struggling cause. [6]

Thinking... but in pictures. Because pictures can make ideas vivid, less abstract, a kind of thinking incarnate. Or they can work as metaphors that offer a new way of seeing an old idea. Then there's Einstein's line: 'If I can't picture it, I can't understand it' (you, me, Bert... same page). So maybe pictures could bring more clarity.

We could call it 'pic-thinking' – like 'quick-thinking' – as you can often take in a picture at a glance. And not only quick, but lasting; images stick in the mind, they're place-holders for more extensive thoughts, and the mind needs something to stick because as neurologists tell us it's made of yoghurt.

That's the big sell, so let's immediately cut it down to size. We all struggle, there are no easy answers to how to think, and we're not about to bring a new dawn of rational and respectful deliberation with a shot of a bike chicane. But given the struggle, all methods to the pump I say. If there are marginal gains to be had, let's have them. That's the story, anyway, and that's how I decided to keep an eye out for pictures that I'd stick above the desk if I wanted a portrait gallery of smart-thinking.

'Sounds like this might even fly,' I thought for nearly ten seconds... Except then came the practicalities. Such as: who's it for then, this picture book?

Partly for those not too steeped in smart-thinking; an intro – or maybe a refresher or stock-take – for anyone wondering what to make of the pile of books. But even the cognoscenti might be curious about the pics, and maybe about the author's two cents, as there are opinions here, too – more on that in a minute. And anyway the problems at the simple end of knowing stuff have a curious way of being the same at the hard end, too. Or maybe the book would appeal to those, like me, curious about how to communicate ideas. While if you think it's a gimmick, that'll be because you're biased and irrational and need a new picture book to set you straight. So that's about everyone, then.

OK, next practicality: pictures of what, exactly?

Not graphs or charts. And not mind-maps or icons or any of the usual diagrammatic visualizations of ideas that you find in business school (with a couple of partial exceptions). That's another book. And no cheesy literality – like illustrating an 'open mind' with a cartoon image of a tin-opened head.[7]

Otherwise, all sorts – old, new, drawings, photos, memes; maybe not spectacular, just hoping to be vivid and useful, and with luck the odd 'aha!' – meaning the choice is bound to be personal. You might see other things in these pictures, or you might see nothing relevant and wonder what the author's been on. If you can find better – and I bet you can – do.

But that slightly ducks the question about what kind of pictures, and this is where things get serious. Bear with me here, because the real issue turns out to be this: if you want to picture an idea, you need to be clear what the idea is. What's its essence?

Obvious, really. But that question – and the surprising difficulty in answering it – entirely shapes this book. It might also help to explain smart-thinking's struggles. Why? Because the more you try to clarify smart-thinking, the more you realize how messy it is.

Too often while thinking about the essence of a smart-thinking idea – how to describe or picture it, if we boil it down – a small, militant voice interrupted, 'Hang on… How reliable is this idea really? Isn't the truth sometimes the opposite?'

Example: motivated reasoning is bad. That's a big theme in smart-thinking. Yet some of the most profoundly good things that ever happened – name a few… female suffrage, the fight against slavery – were surely helped at times by people who grabbed any evidence that served the cause, their reasoning and judgement being fiercely motivated and their minds slammed shut (another supposed Bad Thing), and most of us would find it absurd, even offensive, to say they should have been more open. Less motivated, more open-minded – on slavery?

So, are we sure the bads are reliably bad? David Hume (eighteenth-century thinker) famously seemed to say that the bad of motivated reasoning wasn't bad at all, it was right and proper: 'Reason is, and ought to be the slave of the passions, and can never pretend to any other office than to serve and obey them,' he wrote.[8] And while people argue with Hume or say he didn't mean what he seems to mean, because we can separate legitimately motivated and passionate goals and values ('end slavery!') from how we reason towards them ('now, some coldly rational tactics to achieve abolition…'), you can easily find another thinker who'll tell you that motivation and reasoning are wholly entangled at every stage and bound to be that way.[9]

And yet critics of motivated reasoning describe mixing up motive and reason like it's a thought-crime. And they have a point. Sometimes we're so motivated to find the answer we want that we'll stampede the evidence into the dust for it. So one day motivated reasoning stinks, the next it's OK, maybe good, another it can't be helped. Which? When? Is it possible to use motivation – which we need – without abusing reason? In short, values, passions, motivation and reason... it's complicated. Get into the academic thickets about whether we should idealize value-free science, for example, and you might never emerge.[10]

Similarly, if it's smart to be open-minded, how open-minded must we be towards people who seem malevolent, or just wildly wrong or reek of bad faith? Or should we never assume that until we've talked with an open mind to every last conspiracy theorist? And if we are going to say that some things have manifest clarity, so sod this open-mind business, which, when exactly, under what terms? Sometimes, to make sense of smart-thinking, you need a good philosopher.

There are lots of cases like this and they make smart-thinking messier than it looks; not a manual of technical fixes, but a bunch of hints – some strong, many not, with limits, maybe disputed, conflicting, contextual, nuanced, often tricky to put into use, with devil in the detail. Many a smart-thinking virtue has an opposite virtue; books disagree, of course they do; ideas change. And out in the wild, essences are often elusive. And while few rules are universal – so, in a way, what do you expect? – this is much more than one or two edge cases.

The quickest parallel is with proverbs, which also deal in timeless wisdom, or claim to. 'A stitch in time saves nine,' says one; except another verges on the opposite: 'Look before you leap.'

Oh, thanks, you say: fat use you are, with your wisdom of caution and wisdom of speed. Which? When? Smart-thinking can be similar. Picking its examples carefully, one book tells us – and tells us like it's a slam-dunk – that quick, intuitive thinking is the way to go (*Blink* by Malcolm Gladwell[11]), so trust your gut (but first train it to have the right kind of speedy intuitions); another, that quick-thinking is riddled with bias and ideally you should think more slowly and reflectively (*Thinking, Fast and Slow* by Daniel Kahneman[12]). Blink v. Think, it's been called.

But which, when? Some say we should *Blink* when we have sound experience to inform a snap-judgement; except that others ask how you can know if your experience is sufficient for the problem at hand unless you *Think* first. And while you're mulling over that one, along comes another to say *Don't Trust your Gut*, trust data,[13] (though it says sometimes your gut turns out to be right). Then up pops *The Economist* magazine to tell us that judging when it's right to use gut instinct will often be decided by... gut instinct.[14] Er... right. Does that also mean we must first train our instincts about gut instincts? Wheels within wheels or what?

Confused? Good. Rational reaction if you ask me. The problem is it's all these, like the proverbs. Quick-thinking can be riddled with bias. But quick-thinking – maybe using rules of thumb or trained intuition – can also be brilliantly efficient, even lifesaving, and maybe the only option for flesh-and-blood humans under pressure. Unsurprisingly, experts also find the right choice of *Blink* and *Think* a puzzle.[15] Some cases are easy, many are not.

Here's another. Some smart-thinking tells us that the power of data is how it reveals the facts. True. 'The data don't lie' is a phrase you hear. But other smart-thinking tells us data can be a snake-pit. Also true. Statistics can be treacherous. So there's a balance of both ambition and hazard: using the power of data versus being used by the power of data; loving numbers for their insights or trashing them as lies, damned lies and statistics. Since no number speaks for itself, how deep must we go to know which is which, especially when many are both at the same time? Some numbers are easy to see through, many aren't.

Likewise, we'll see traps in reading too much into the results of chance, and in reading too little and overlooking its power to change everything; we'll see the wonder in simplification, and the jeopardy; the genius in spotting patterns and the delusion. For example, Marcus du Sautoy writes in *Thinking Better* about the huge value of pattern-spotting, citing the stock market as a case in point; Nassim Taleb writes in *The Black Swan* about the huge *risks* of pattern-spotting, citing the stock market as a case in point.

You can even finish up wondering if the very exhortation to think smart or be sceptical could be double-edged and partly responsible for the current popularity of conspiracy theories, or self-anointed citizen scientists who decide after an evening online that they know more about Covid-19 than the virologists.

What this messiness tells us is that while smart-thinking ideas make sense *sometimes*, at other times they can easily fail or be misapplied. But the worst of it is how we can know which of those times we're in: is this one when smart-thinking idea X rules or not? Or put it another way: smart-thinking has great answers if only we can be sure of the question. Trouble is, life doesn't define its questions for us on our terms; it doesn't present its problems pre-labelled to suit the fixes we already have in mind. All of which is to say that smart-thinking may be smart but, in the unforgiving noise of life, it's often close to screw-up.

How close? Perilously close. There are two nasty facts here with implications for smart-thinking that some of it hasn't clocked. First, even the most trained, acclaimed modern thinking has a horribly mixed track record. The replication crisis noted a few pages back has seen too many findings in science – including medicine – fail to stand up when retested (some always fail, but the level of failure has been too systematic for comfort, not something you can put down to chance). The reckoning has so far been most severe in psychology – exactly where smart-thinking science began in the 1970s. Why are the findings failing? The list is long. There's soul-searching about everything from statistical competence in research to how experiments are designed, the quality of causal inferences drawn from data, research and publishing incentives, transparency, honesty and fraud, you name it, including a failure to self-correct efficiently. One writer-researcher – and not on the lunatic fringe, but credible and mainstream – says much of the scientific process is 'deeply corrupted'. [16]

Just to point out the obvious here: this is science. This is elite smart-thinking, often highly numerate and skilled at finding things out. And it's frequently, dangerously, unfit for purpose. Amos Tversky said: 'Whenever there is a simple problem that most laymen fall for, there is always a slightly more sophisticated version of the same problem that experts fall for.' [17] The replication crisis is the disaster movie of that quote. And by the way, some say there's a new replication crisis on the way in artificial intelligence and machine learning. [18] And while a huge amount of science is also robust and wonderful, and in the long run discovering faults should help because we can now improve how we do it, for those who say scientific method is our salvation it's a pain, as it shows how easily smart method is corruptible, too – consciously or not. So when trying to explain why we know stuff, the answer 'Because... science' is often not good enough. Which is intimidating. Because if science is often not good enough, how smart do we have to be?

And just to complicate things in case they're not already, the ideas kicking around to improve science are as much about smartening systems as individuals; about how research is organized, incentivized and published, because people in a bad system can read all the smarts they like and be no further on. Thinking is not simply a private affair.[19]

Second nasty fact: smart-thinking itself isn't immune to suddenly falling into doubt long after being all the rage. Example: one breakthrough of the last decade – 'nudge theory' – now faces the suspicion that published research into how well it works was skewed in its favour, among other doubts.[20] While this doesn't prove it useless, it could be far less powerful than claimed, though nudgers will no doubt fight back. Another example: a whole slate of cognitive biases known as priming and stated as facts by one of the smart-thinking bibles has turned out suspect.[21]

Bluntly, then, smart-thinking can be disputed or even plain wrong (controversial opinion: I thought *Noise*, Daniel Kahneman and others' latest, hugely acclaimed smart-thinking blockbuster half right, but basically half wrong[22]).

Another hitch, maybe the worst: the very idea that we can train people in general smarts is in doubt. Read this from a recent research paper and wonder if the whole enterprise is doomed:

Considerable research has been carried out in the last two decades on the putative benefits of cognitive training on cognitive function and academic achievement. Recent meta-analyses... have led to a crystal-clear conclusion: the overall effect of far transfer is null ['far transfer' means how well the lessons turn into general skills that people can use in new contexts; 'null' means nothing, zero, i.e. they don't]... Despite these conclusions, the field has maintained an unrealistic optimism about the cognitive and academic benefits of cognitive training... We demonstrate that this optimism is due to the field neglecting the results of meta-analyses and largely ignoring the statistical explanation that apparent effects are due to a combination of sampling errors and other artifacts.[23]

Ouch! Not least because the claim here is that assessments of the value of cognitive training were themselves cognitively weak. Kinda funny, no? Or sad. One or two other credible verdicts are less gloomy,[24] but hardly gushing; and yes, this is 'cognitive training', not 'smart-thinking', but if you think they're different enough not to overlap, you're overthinking.

Not for a millisecond, by the way, am I anti-science or research, or smarter thinking. The question is how to do it all better. But the trouble with that is it leads us ever deeper into wonk territory, where in science, for example, it's about which incentives encourage better-quality research, and what analytical methods and experimental designs work best for what purposes – and that hurts even to say it. For the rest of us, this becomes an ever less-accessible, technical swamp of high-end expertise. For we wannabe writers, it's similarly bad news: if full-blooded science struggles to think clearly, to make sense of evidence properly, to work out what's up and how to find out, what chance pop science can do it? All of which makes you wonder if smart-thinking raises our expectations too high, raises our sense of sophistication more than the substance and just makes us smug.

Bottom line: this business often starts easy, but gets hard, fast. And yet, strangely, the books are not nearly so good at exploring their limits. If you don't realize this early on, smart-thinking might turn you into one more arrogant jackass, except now with added jargon and more books. Sorry, did you come here for simple answers reduced to pretty pictures? Course not, you're smarter than that.

Even so, you're not here to be told our efforts are futile, and there'd be little point in a book like this that declared itself a waste of time. So what do we do about the messiness, and how will this book help?

The upshot for the smart-thinking ideas themselves is not that they're necessarily wrong or useless – they can be brilliant, and sometimes simple – but we need to recognize their status as ideas, often artful as much as technical,[25] often contested, vulnerable to error and revision, and use them flexibly, with humility, sensitive to context, trying to balance their inconsistent strengths and weaknesses by coming at problems from different sides, always aware of their limitations and ours.[26]

The upshot for this book? Mainly it left me feeling that the most pressing need in smart-thinking is to use it – but to watch it, especially to watch our expectations. Some smart-thinking has always been like this, sceptical, hesitant, warning of overconfidence, and this book shares that emphasis, maybe pushes it, with a nervous streak about smart-thinking itself.

And the upshot for the pictures? At first I wondered if the messiness might wreck the whole scheme, until it occurred to me that pictures could be pretty good at illustrating mess and ambiguity. They bring it to life, showing the tricky detail and context where the action often is. The problem is that smart-thinking can sound too clean, but when we *see* what it has to work on, that brings home the truth of one of my favourite book titles of all time: *I Think You'll Find it's a Bit More Complicated Than That.*[27] Pictures can help us see both the ambition in smart-thinking and the potential gremlins, by showing us ideas in the wild. They too are often riffs on 'use it, but watch it', trying to be constructive as we attempt to bring out more of the awkward trade-offs and practical realism of seeing it how it is.

And one more point worth stressing: it's easy to see all this as an inconvenience, a pain even. My advice is to resist that mood. It is too defeatist. If you think you like smart-thinking and not merely the reputation for it, then you should relish the act of thinking. Complication is hard, but inherently interesting. So don't feel intimidated. Dive in.

In practice, each chapter picks a theme in smart-thinking – usually with a sceptical edge, because that's my own bias – then adds a picture to suggest how it works in the wild, includes a few stories or examples, then throws in a few simple challenges to try to make you think again, and not just nod. You'll find one chapter points your thinking this way, another that. Sometimes a chapter goes both ways at once. All include objections to their own main theme. And, frankly, tough. Few all-purpose basics work every time.

Have this thought tattooed somewhere: *There is no royal road to truth or reason*. The biggest difference between this book and some of its kind – apart from the pictures – is how itchy it is about answers, all of them, including its own. Its paradoxical message is that too many case studies in the smart-thinking lit are too neat, and this stuff is often messy, so we need simple ways to see how. The overall aim, I decided, would be to be unsettling, but not paralysing,[28] to use smart-thinking while doubting it. All told, a tall order, but here goes.

Now you realize you're not in for an easy answer, it could be tempting to turn cynic, ranting on your way out that nothing works. Not clever. Cynicism is useless and boring. If your only trick is destruction – and cynicism does nothing but knock things down – then you soon live in a ruin. And anyway cynicism is nothing like scepticism. Healthy scepticism is more like a workshop where we put competing ideas to the test – both the ideas we don't like and the ideas we do, testing them equally – knowing that in the end they can all be flawed, but we must still make decisions.[29]

It's like having dragonfly eyes, one of the best of the books says,[30] seeing through many lenses at once, taking none for granted. How does a problem look using this piece of smart-thinking? Hold that. Now how about if we see it with another? OK, so which way do we fly? If there's one metaphor that new readers could take to heart before diving in, I'd make it dragonfly eyes. You'll hear about them often. Here's a picture. Stick it above the desk.

Dragonfly eyes make smart-thinking as much about attitude, judgement, uncertainty and trade-offs as how to spot a cognitive bias. There's not one easy path to the light; instead, we move towards the best trade-off we can find, making bets, arguing, using flawed evidence and imperfect strategies. Smart-thinking gives us ideas, that's all; how to use them at

If anybody... by any so-called objective thinking, imagines they can conquer doubt, they are mistaken.

Søren Kierkegaard

The dragonfly view. From Joshua van Kleef, Richard Berry and Gert Stange, 'Directional Selectivity in the Simple Eye of an Insect', *Journal of Neuroscience*, 12 March 2008.

any moment is our own balancing act – no book can do that for us.

Thinking in Pictures aims to give you a few of these ideas as memorably as it can, but adds danger signs and alternatives, then encourages you to weigh them all up. That means being sceptical of this book, too. The truth is – and don't I know it – that it, too, could be wrong in a hundred ways. But if you want pat answers that work every time, you're looking in not just the wrong book, but the wrong world.

I've also thrown in a few playful exercises and a steer into those other books, if the curiosity takes you – because the books often do say good stuff... mostly. And this is a short book that doesn't pretend to say it all.[31]

So that's it: pics, big themes from the world of smart-thinking, my two cents. You can go now, look at the pictures.[32]

Try this

Just as a run out, to get into the habit, take the dragonfly view to heart... and come up with a few reasons why it's a bad steer. That's right: argue with me.

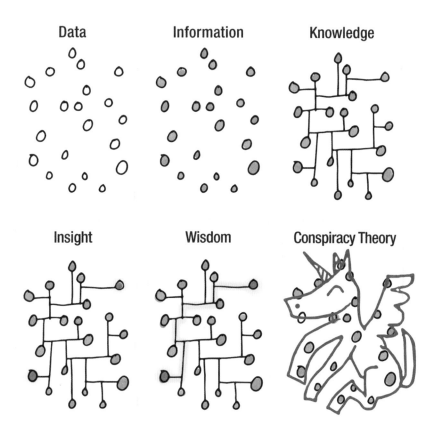

Stop making sense. The original image (boxes 2 and 3) was by Hugh MacLeod at the design consultancy Gaping Void, who sent it to their email list, where it acquired a life of its own.

2

Unjoin your dots

First, you

There's a story that still bothers me from more than thirty years ago. I was a newbie reporter for a provincial newspaper when a guy came in with a haunted look and a revelation to 'blow the lid off' County Hall.

Social services were plotting to kill him.

'They're taking over my mind.'

'Wow,' I said, searching his face.

They were forcing him to drive into oncoming traffic; he could feel the temptation, he said, and his hands mimed a slow turn of the wheel.

First thought? 'Sh*t! Is this guy actually on the road? He could die.'

Second thought: '*I* could die.'

Then he said: 'The police told me I was paranoid.'

'They did?'

'But you'd be paranoid if someone was trying to kill you.'

... and I thought: 'Hang on, that actually makes sense. Yes, yes, you would be paranoid if someone was trying to kill you.' And yes, I know it's an old joke, but I think he was sincere.

He'd joined the dots.

Joining the dots is what we say we do when we put together pieces of evidence to work out what's up. 'Join the dots!' people urge, when they think we're failing to catch on. That's what smart people do, they join the dots.

Good. Except... even the most delusional have an internal logic based on evidence of some kind. Everyone does. Some of it really might be logical. We're all joining the dots – you, me, my man – connecting information, looking for pattern and meaning, and when we think we've found it, we think we've found it. 'You're so naive,' a guy said to my partner when she had her Covid jab. He'd joined the dots. So had she.

That should be troubling. It means, on the money or deluded, rational or not, professor or loon (or maybe both), on the inside it all feels the same. Do you trust that feeling? Why? Because you're clever?

As we talked, my man struck me as clever. His cleverness was worse than useless. It helped him justify joining his dots. All he really knew was that the dots made sense to him. It's all any of us knows to begin with, and it's often not much. We're quick to see patterns and meaning, quick to find reasons why one thing connects with another; it's a kind of human genius, but it treads on thin ice. Once suspected, patterns real and imagined are absurdly easy for the clever to think they can confirm; once we unleash our amazing powers of reasoning, everything can be made to fit. As Richard McElreath of the Max Planck Institute once said: 'Never rely on being clever.'[1]

OK, thanks for the warning, you say, but I still think I can spot a pink flying unicorn when I see one (thus instantly relying on being clever, duh!). Sure about that?

> *We don't have to go the whole they're-trying-to-kill-me conspiracy hog to move past the wisdom box into delusion. We do it in a thousand small ways. As the books tell you, the list of human fallibilities is long: memory can be a fantasist, perception is easily duped*

(see optical illusions) and, maybe worst of all, people are said to be a wandering fog of cognitive biases that distort evidence. There are dozens of these biases and the books go on about them, some are about nothing else; but just one bias makes the point, the biggest and simplest, and you might already know it: confirmation bias (closely related to 'myside bias'). It goes a little like this: we gleefully seize evidence that confirms what we already think or want to believe, and find reasons to dismiss whatever doesn't.

Easy to see the potential tension with truth. As one member of the rational-thinking royalty put it: 'Of the fifty-odd biases discovered... forty-nine are cute quirks, and one is destroying civilization. This last one is confirmation bias.' That's a little harsh on the forty-nine, but has the priority right. The 'destroying civilization' line is because confirmation bias supposedly makes civil-war partisans of us all. Whatever our side, we find evidence to confirm we're right. Next thing, we decide the other lot must be idiots or evil.[2]

Smart-thinkers argue about whether we're stuck with our cognitive glitches – less *Homo sapiens*, more Homer Simpson, said one[3] – or can learn to see past them. Let's glide over all that and say that, right now, doesn't matter. All we need agree at this stage is that we're highly fallible – at perpetual risk of seeing pink unicorns – and that's one thing most smart-thinkers do agree on, or they'd be out of a job. It's true this only gets us so far; it doesn't tell us what to do about our fallibility. But still, it's a vital step. Without it, nothing jolts our tendency to self-regard – and our self-regard needs jolting daily.

This is a recurrent theme in smart-thinking: the need to give cosy presumptions a repeated kick. The books almost all say it. You see it so often it's tedious. But that's another danger – that we think we're now well placed to do the kicking, we grow complacent, we know this, we're clever, we've read the books...

That is, the jolt must be never-ending. Looking for a picture to give it, I chose this one because it tricks us, playing to our vanity only on further reflection to laugh at us. Did you look at the sequence of pictures – how data can be turned into knowledge, and knowledge into wisdom – and think, 'Yeah, yeah, so true... ' And then did you laugh at the joke in the last frame that sets apart the wise who know all this (i.e. you) from the conspiracist fools and all those other wackos – and did you smile because you know which side you're on, being clever. And so did you congratulate yourself on being the kind of rationalist who doesn't cross the line into the unicorn box? Well, did ya, punk?

Excellent. Because you just outed yourself as one more of the deluded. So did I, as that was my first instinct. We all like to think we've earned our place in the wisdom box, more or less, but we're all liable to bias, misjudgement and complacency, meaning that we're the joke. Told twice to begin with self-reflection – 'unjoin **your** dots', 'first, **you**' – you still looked and smirked at how this picture mocked someone else. So wrong again, sucker on your own hype, because as far as I'm concerned, it mocks you and me, and we didn't see it. We joined the wrong dots even as we basked in joining the right ones.

On reflection, maybe my man and I were not so far apart. Maybe high-status, peer-reviewed science from august institutions published in big-name journals that turns out to be questionable is sometimes not far apart, either. Maybe smart-thinking, too.

In other words, one of the best acts of scepticism for the budding smart-thinker is to be sceptical of your own smart-thinking and reading – including this book, and all the books.

So make this picture your reminder of the often-scary proximity of wisdom and flying unicorns, rationality, irrationality, obvious and fake, logic and error; how there are dangers everywhere and one of the worst is our own ever-so-smart reasoning, but how we hate to think this means me. As a poet once said: 'Nothing dies harder than the desire to think well of oneself.'[4]

(Here we're coming to the point, so brace yourself.) Until we shout our fallibility out loud – not just as a truth about 'people', but about you and me, personally, at every unsuspecting moment, however clever we are – we won't try to fix it. 'My name's Michael and I see pink flying unicorns.' Your turn.

Once said, this changes everything. Because even if it doesn't give us the answers to what we should think, saying it matters, because it changes the question. The problem now becomes not what we know and the sense we make of the world, or think we do, but how we verify what we think we know. Because otherwise, how do we know that what we think we know isn't pink and airborne? That's a huge shift in effort and attention. Epistemologists – they who get philosophical about how we claim to know anything – sometimes talk about it as the problem of 'reliability'.[5]

Pretty soon we realize this means the hack of all hacks is how to recognize reliable ways of knowing, reliable sources and reliable people, because knowledge means nothing if it comes from reading tea leaves.[6] Reliability, in my book, is not far short of everything (though to make life really messy, it's often not black and white; reliability comes in degrees – see later chapters). Lack of reliability is where the science replication crisis came from.

This in turn raises the intimidating spectre of trying to tell high- from low-quality evidence, and good from not-so-good research methods. Strangely, research methods don't light many people's fires. They're also easily done wrong, and quickly become complicated. But while this will emphatically not be a textbook about research method, there's just no avoiding it: 'How do they know that? What's the quality of the finding out? Is it rigorous?' are among my first questions about almost any claim or info beyond a road sign.

We'll talk later about the best ways we non-specialists can judge if the finding out is kosher. But tell me you know what you know because you 'did your own research', and I hope you don't mean you went on Google ('Google knowing') and looked for people to prove you right (more confirmation bias). Is that your method? So, we have work to do.

And it starts with you: you first and only, and you on the inside, not how you look or sound, not about your group/team/party/side and how you fit in. Forget all that external stuff for a moment if you can (you won't, but you can try). And it's not about your opponents. If you want to think well, get humble, get reflective, get curious and serious about how *you* think. You can sort everyone else's stupidity later.

> Brandishing smart credentials is just asking the cosmic-irony fairy for a kick in the pants. One of the best kicks – though a lot of people lost a lot of money – was in late 2022 when the FTX Future Fund (an investment fund with a focus on existential risk, and with links to the

rational-thinking community) underestimated the existential risk to... itself. It went spectacularly bust.[7]

The first task in smart-thinking then, the place much of it begins, is to distinguish ego from reason. It's also the hardest, as ego can eat reason between meals and you might never notice. Develop a nit-picking, sceptical self-awareness, the books imply, or it's cognitive death by ego. A recent book on the theme was simply called *Know Thyself*.[8]

Here are three big-name smart-thinkers practising biasology: spotting and analysing other people's biases – in this case about Covid-19 when the virus hit the West early in 2020. But were they as cool, rational and bias-free as they'd like us to think?

1 *Cass Sunstein, co-author of* Nudge, *under the headline 'The Cognitive Bias That Makes Us Panic About Coronavirus': 'At this stage, no one can specify the magnitude of the threat from the coronavirus. But one thing is clear: A lot of people are more scared than they have any reason to be.' He blamed a bias called probability neglect: 'Suppose that residents of a midsize city are alarmed about the risk, perhaps because false rumours are flying, perhaps because one person or a few people in the area have been diagnosed with the coronavirus. It is likely that for residents of that city, the risk of infection is really low and much lower than risks to which they are accustomed in ordinary life – say, the risk of getting the flu, pneumonia or strep throat.' (This was before vaccines arrived.)*

2 *Paul Slovic, a giant on risk who I've read for decades, quoted in the* New York Times *under the headline 'Coronavirus "Hits all the Hot Buttons" for How We Misjudge Risk'. 'Our feelings don't do arithmetic very well,' he said. People focus on fatalities and not the '98% or so of people who are recovering from it and may have mild cases.' We overreact.*

3 *Gerd Gigerenzer, another giant whose books I love, who said that only with hindsight would we know if we had over- or underreacted to Covid-19, but then compared it to swine flu and terrorism, stressing how few of us those actually hurt. He said we should approach problems like Covid-19 'with a cooler head'. We needed better risk literacy, he said. Headline: 'Why What Does Not Kill Us Makes Us Panic'.*[9]

Do the above three belong in the wisdom box? Or did they cross the unicorn line? Despite caveats, all three saw panic and overreaction. Whatever your own views, I suspect even they wonder if they got it right. Did we overreact or underreact, or both? Maybe governments were slow, plenty of us were complacent and some paid with their lives, while to compare Covid (200,000+ dead in the UK, about one million in the US) with strep-throat seems a little off, don't you think? Which is why I'm a little doubtful these bias and risk-illiteracy spotters were as clear-sighted as they thought. But if calling out bias is your hammer, maybe you see these nails everywhere. Maybe that's your bias. Out in the wild, even the tools that show us how people are fallible... are fallible.

'If only they (who disagree with me) weren't so cognitively

biased, they'd see how right I was' seems to be how this piece of smart-thinking usually plays. Pretty sure I've thought the same from time to time. Suffice to say, knowing more about cognitive biases hasn't been the breakthrough to objectivity once hoped.

I still say the three thinkers here are super-smart. I still say: read them. But we can all – even the smartest – easily cross the line; while bias-ology (like all smart-thinking) can turn out insightful or self-deluding: just us joining our favourite dots.[10]

Not so fast

OK, all very worthy, but... on several counts, pulling in differ-ent ways. Ready with your dragonfly eyes?

1. First, the dots do need joining somehow. We can't escape judgement for ever. What if self-awareness and self-questioning turn you into a self-obsessed, inde-cisive, ineffectual value-vacuum who doesn't know what to think or do, but just sits weighing alternatives?

2. Next, are we sure ego is the enemy of smart-thinking? Sometimes a little confidence helps with independent thinking. Think smart-thinking books are humble and free of ego? Some are the most massively self-assured things I've ever read. There's a potential contradiction written through the idea of humble smart-thinking, right from the start.

3. More fundamentally, no one can unjoin all their dots to observe life with no structure (moral,

ideological...) whatsoever. It's been called the 'view from nowhere', but we all start somewhere. Doesn't mean we can't *try* to be neutral, and certainly doesn't mean we should encourage all thinking – science included – to become more partisan. But we need to temper the ideal with what's achievable: not a world without prior beliefs, maybe a willingness to look them harder in the mirror. But that first box, the pure data box, all dots floating free and objective? Doesn't exist, as we'll see shortly.

4. In fact, final objection: if it's true we're that fallible, what hope of thinking well at all, especially when so many books suggest humanity is irrational and dumb – 'a caveman out of time', as the author and psychologist Steven Pinker describes that view?[11] Take these objections together and the chance of doing it even half right can feel squeezed to zero: objectivity can't be had, the rest is Neanderthal. Shall we give up?

But if our thinking was that bad, we'd struggle to cross a road. We wouldn't have reduced maternal mortality in developed countries in the last 200 years from about 800 per 100,000 women to five per 100,000.[12] If rationality is hopeless, what's the point of democracy, argument, science, except as vanity? Stephen Poole writes, 'reasoning is the social institution whose reliability underwrites all the other kinds of civil and political institutions of civilized life'.[13] Note, civilized life, not pond life.

So, let's have some proportion. Yes, even science can be corrupted and has acts of hideous confirmation bias and lousy reasoning. Even science is full of vanity and littered with bad incentives. We're all, every one of us, capable of the existentially bad call. So if we don't believe we're highly fallible, we are the problem. But fallible does not equal hopeless. We still learn, still discover things unimagined; there is abundant evidence that people do attend to the facts, not simply their prejudices – of course they do; if an HGV is hurtling towards us, we get out of the way, not insist it'll all be fine because that would be more convenient. Truth is often out there and, when we see it, we often know it. There is a unicorn box, it's true, but there is also a wisdom box – both.

There's a strand of smart-thinking that I think of as the rationality wars: people are basically dumb; oh no they're not, in practice they're pretty smart; oh yes they are dumb, but they could be clever if they read my book. My conclusion is more boring: there's a chance of thinking well for all of us, is what I'm saying, a hope, but failure is also right there. It's precarious, folks, that's all, and no less so after you've read the books. As a small start, stick the dots and the unicorn above your desk to show both the hope and your own cognitive *memento mori* in pink, cheek-by-jowl. Also, if you think you're a fearless sceptic, prove it: start on you.

Postscript

What happened with the guy? I seem to remember a pitiful effort on my part to sound helpful without fanning his delusions, and then his sadness after I couldn't promise him the front page. Was I part of the conspiracy? He said he was fighting the mind control and resisting, which was mildly reassuring,

I guess. Was it a hoax? I wondered. But turned out he was already on official radars, so if he was conning me, he was conning them, but I think not. In the end, I hoped he received the help he needed to unjoin his dots. Should I have done more? Looking back, yes. Never saw or heard from him again and didn't write the story – until now. Mercifully, there were no reports of strange car crashes.

Try this

Julia Galef (*The Scout Mindset*) suggests a series of self-tests for our neatly joined dots. A few are below. Her book, which I like, describes others.

- *The selective sceptic test*: would I find a rhetorical trick, style of argument or type of evidence quite so persuasive if used by the other side? Or is my scepticism selective?

- *The double-standard test*: do I hold myself to the standard of argument that I demand of others?

- *The outsider test:* think of someone whose reasoning I respect as independent, not tribal, and ask myself if they'd come to the same conclusion.

- *The ideological Turing test*: if I think I really know an opponent's views or reasons, could I argue those reasons to someone else and sound like a believer?

- And one more in the same vein that I like, from

Jennifer Saul via Philip Tetlock: *the fig-leaf test.* Are you just adept at finding fig leaves for your friends and tearing them off your enemies?

Jargon

- *Metacognition*: thinking about how we think. Prized by smart-thinkers.

- *The principle of charity*: giving credit to your opponents by taking the strongest interpretation of their argument and motives. Aka steel-manning, in contrast to straw-manning.

3

Un-count your sheep

Data ain't nature

So, as we were saying: sheep. How many?

Two. Obvs. Next question.

Or...

... maybe one?

Because one's a lamb, not a sheep? Although saying that... aren't lambs sheep?

OK, I see this depends on whether you want to be awkward or clever or whatever, or maybe you'd call it precise, or perhaps it depends on why you're counting – say, because you're a farmer who needs to know how many full-size fleeces you'll have this year; or how many of the flock will be ready for slaughter and no one eats mutton these days (don't think about it); or I don't know why, because I know nothing about farming, or sheep...[1]

In which case... one and a half?

Although maybe the ewe is pregnant and about to give birth again in the next ten seconds (it's not, but run with this), so how many sheep now? Three? One and two halves? Two and one half? Two? One plus a half plus a quarter? Still one? Though now we're about it, that's a pretty big lamb. Are we sure that's a lamb?

Oh, come *on*! There are two white woolly things in this picture, can we not agree?

No, maybe we can't. Counting just got tricky after one.

Why does it matter about two sheep (approximately) in a Welsh field? Because this is where it all begins. When people talk about what's up in the world, how do they know? Because they think they have evidence, and that evidence is often data, numbers, measurement, counting. And often they're right, or right enough. But bear in mind that for every number, every piece of data, every statistic, every claim there's more of this or that, every medicinal drug that's assessed to work or not, every economic trend – unemployment, GDP, poverty – every measured comparison, every quantified risk... in fact, whenever anything is counted or measured in the real world, *someone decides* what to count and how.

Who is the someone? Why decide like that?

Here's the point: you can't avoid numbers if you want to know stuff. And counting in abstract (as in one, two, three) is easy. Because it's also true in some way, it sounds objective. Note: *the world is not like this.*

Counting real things in the wild is about much more than counting. It's about gritty, messy practicalities with dirt under their hooves and fingernails, and how we force the world into neat, countable categories. (For an example of numbers that sound like the most natural thing in the world, but aren't, try Hasok Chang's *Inventing Temperature*.)

Think this obvious? Think everyone knows the importance of what goes into the analytical sausage machine, what the vast, super-smart world of data analytics sometimes calls data quality or data design? Sick of the adage 'garbage-in-garbage-out' (GIGO), because you know it already?

Then why, as no less than Google's chief decision scientist points out, is there no job title that recognizes the essential role of data quality on which the whole shebang depends?

'Riddle me this,' says Cassie Kozyrkov: 'If we have a whole industry of GIGO-respecting professionals and we also understand that designing quality datasets isn't trivial, where's the evidence that we put our money where our mouths are?' That is, whose job is it to make sure the data's up to it? No one seems clear, she says.[2]

So you might think that all this is bottom-rung smarts, but it stays awkward all the way to the top, however many books you've read. Almost whoever you are, it's worth some sheep (one, one and half?) above the desk.

One key to the problem is that counting is as much about descriptive words and categories, the labels we choose to attach to what we count and why – sheep or lamb? – as it is about numbers. These labels are ours not nature's, and that means counting is also about power – the power to decide what we count and how and what labels to use – and so it's about existing beliefs and habits and prejudices and assumptions, plus the boring practicalities of how you actually do the counting, which can all shape our decisions, to the extent that counting *something* becomes the soft centre of 99 per cent of the statistics known to humankind, all the way up to the data used to train artificial intelligence or machine learning.

I don't mean nothing in nature divides into discrete or countable things, or that every category is a lie. Some categories work well enough and have an underlying reality. Others really show their human fingerprints. Even counting to one in real life can be harder than it sounds, and many of the data that we see and hear, and often accept, are quietly struggling with – or ignoring – this devilish detail. But it's a detail that can change everything. Data are not just out there, they're co-created by us, and that act of creation needs scrutiny. It all begins (all this numbers stuff, every last crumb) shaped by people.[3]

> So, labels and categories. When a headline said one in four boys was a yob – what a survey had called 'a serious or persistent offender' – what did the labels mean? Turned out 'offender' could mean tripping or pushing someone. And, deliciously, the someone could be your brother. That is, pushing your bro' could put you in the same category as violent assault. In this survey everyone was a sheep, no lambs defined. The miracle is that only one in four boys met the definition.[4]

A quick picture reminder that categories and labels are made by people to serve their other purposes, with a category labelled 'Bangladesh'. This particular piece of that category, known as the Tin Bigha gap, owes little to nature and everything to what people wanted or needed it to be, after long negotiation: a small, guarded corridor of sovereignty 178 metres long x 85 metres wide, surrounded by and leased from India, connecting one piece of Bangladesh with another (entrance shown below). There were enclaves of Bangladesh (cyan and dots) and India (orange and dots) all along the border until about 2015, when they tidied things up, leaving just the Tin Bigha gap. That's categories for you: often, very human.

The point sounds trivial. It's routinely ignored because it sounds trivial. But it's stupefying when we realize how much this triviality matters. How many sophisticates have paraded a number that turned out to be categorized in sand or labelled with intent? Don't know what's worse: when they know it or when they don't.

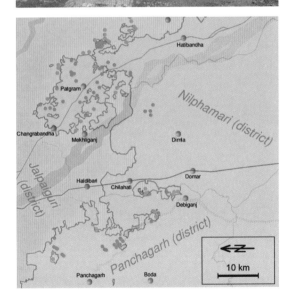

Try these examples for more definitional joy...

In summer 2021 the UK government committed to building 'forty new hospitals'. What kind of category or label do you reckon 'new hospital' is? Turned out a new wing or major refurbishment was a 'new hospital'. Later the programme included 'already being built' and 'needs a new roof'. Sheep? Lambs? With numbers, words matter.

A BBC headline, 'Covid: disabled people account for six in 10 deaths in England last year', had a picture of someone in a wheelchair. Pictures, eh? Because now we know what 'disabled people' means. Means wheelchair. But 'disabled' here actually means any long-term limitation to daily activities, even if due to old age. So was Covid hitting the disabled harder or was it hitting the elderly? Almost the same number of non-Covid deaths also meet this definition.

In 2020 the UK's Office for National Statistics said recorded GDP growth of, say, 0.3 per cent in one quarter (three months) might typically be out by... 0.3 per cent, up or down – and we've no idea which. Why so vague? Because the thing we are counting (what's going on in the whole economy) might change in ways we're slow to catch up with, meaning that we only know roughly what the thing is that we're meant to be counting. Few of the big brains that talk about GDP acknowledge quite how hard it is to count something as changeable as an economy, and so they persistently underestimate the uncertainty in the numbers.

What these cases have in common is muddle or mischief about what the counted thing is. This suggests a sense-check for anything counted: picture it. (Try picturing 'the economy' and you realize how elusive the quantification of that thing is.) I owe two of these three examples to David Spiegelhalter, who called his book *The Art of Statistics* because art is what it is – an art of interpretation and judgement – not a science of hard facts. You can find oodles of examples in every popular book about data, stats and numbers in the news. David also tells the fabulous story that you can be dead in one US state but not next door, according to how certification of death is defined.

The result is that if you want to know what's out there, get curious about how we count. Never forget that very first step, when the mess of life is turned into the numbers, statistics and data we use to describe it. This is not the only thing with numbers by a long way, but it's the most common, most fundamental, most easily overlooked. The sheep picture is your essential reminder – it confronts human data with nature – because if we want to know a number's pedigree, know what it's really worth, we should stand in that field (there's an old saying that the best economists have dirt on their shoes).

Another way of putting this: every number has a backstory. But do you know it? Or are you too busy being impressed by the massive sophistication of the analysis by the big-name university, research institute, consultancy or government – whose secret is that although they did the number-crunching and did it brilliantly, the counting *something* where it all started is as woolly as a sheep.

Even artificial intelligence, which can sometimes see deeper than people can know, learns from data, not nature, trained to see what it sees using the ways people already see and count – because what else is there? This data can be as sheep and lamb as all other data.

An example that I first picked up from Abeba Birhane, a researcher I follow: software used across the United

States to predict future criminal behaviour, by counting.... what, exactly? Whatever it counted, it was alleged to be starkly biased against black defendants, taking a more optimistic view of white behaviour (labelling it less risky) and a more pessimistic view of African American behaviour (more risky) than later events justified. The company concerned disputed that. ProPublica, which conducted the investigation, insisted it was correct.

Prediction Fails Differently for Black Defendants		
	WHITE	AFRICAN AMERICAN
Labeled Higher Risk, But Didn't Re-Offend	23.5%	44.9%
Labeled Lower Risk, Yet Did Re-Offend	47.7%	28.0%

Source: ProPublica.

That little table started a big debate on what's sometimes called 'algorithmic fairness'. It's been cited thousands of times.[5] What I take from it above all is that numbers don't exist outside their social context. They're not pure. They don't rise above the messiness of life. Used badly, they end up reinforcing existing prejudice and bias, in algorithms, in machine learning and everywhere else. Algorithms (all that means is a formula for a decision) sound like the apex of cleverness, but they're partly just a mirror – that's how Hannah Fry describes them (see the 'Read On' section on page 295) – and can lead to bad decisions simply by reflecting our misshapen view of reality back to us, biases and all. They don't reflect nature; they reflect existing, people-fashioned data. And we might never know how as it's often a trade secret.

A tip: if you can, before attempting anything serious with data, consult domain experts who know what the data are talking about. For example, if you're looking at medical numbers, ask a relevant doctor if the numbers make sense amid the blood and guts on a busy day, or whatever field they're meant to describe.

But there is another idea lurking under this problem of what data tell you about nature, and it's this: data on their own actually tell you nothing. Nowt. *Nada*. I mean that in this sense: how things are, and why, can never be answered from data alone.[6] You can't do anything with a number until you attach meanings to it. Until then, it's just an abstraction, signifying nothing. Once you accept that – once you acknowledge how much other stuff you need to know or are already unconsciously assuming about the data before you try to make them useful – you realize what a tangled web all information sits in; how much context, theory and practicality it all depends on before we can use it for any purpose whatsoever. So the answer to 'how many sheep?' is: it depends. Tell me more about what you want to know and why – and then let's talk. As Arvind Narayanan, a computer-science professor at Princeton, says: 'Behind the facade of sophisticated formulas and regressions there are usually crude assumptions about the world and datasets whose politics haven't been interrogated. It's important to get to that layer in order to understand any statistic that you come across. Stripped of this context, numbers by themselves have no meaning.'[7]

Not so fast

First, in case you're tempted to think all algorithms are biased crap, check out the example of mortgage lending in America, which it's argued has become *less* biased as credit scoring has become more automated. You heard me... *more* automated, *less* biased (though still far from perfect).[8]

More generally, data ain't nature, true enough, but here's the thing: once you're done with all your counting scepticism, the question still stands. YOU STILL HAVE TO COUNT THE SHEEP!

So come on, how many? You're not off that hook. And when you've answered, work out how you're going to present your answer, and how you'll use it.

We do this because although data ain't nature, it can be a clue. Clue enough to be useful anyway. Or, to put it another way, data are the most compromised evidence out there, apart from all the other kinds. Done badly, it's all bad. Done well, there's a chance, is all I'm saying.[9] And we must take our chances and do the best we can with what we have. This means we have a choice: say it's all dodgy and throw up our hands in despair or, better, put on our boots, get in that field and make the best of it.

That is, you can't ignore numbers because some are dodgy. The 'I found something not right, so I don't believe any of it' school is as daft as believing everything. How can you know about climate change without data? By looking out the window (though that too is a data point)? What'll you do: dismiss whole piles of argument because you find one glitch in one supporting number? Error-spotting sure feels good, but if you think one error is conclusive, you become an error of judgement yourself. Behave like that and nothing survives. How do we know if therapeutic drugs work, without measuring their effects? Or will you refuse to be treated with anything that a pharma company makes money from because that makes its numbers suspect? Congratulations: your purity just raised your chance of dying early.

So never be tempted to scorn numbers as lies and damned lies simply because some are, or because you find flaws. Data and numbers are a must – powerful, revelatory, frequently indispensable, often the best tool we have for working out what's up. But they're also fragile, partial and can be plain wrong. So we look not for certainty or easy answers or infallible methods, because there aren't any, but judgement with imperfect evidence. Often flawed then, numbers might still tell us something – and the task is to discover what. So don't dismiss them; do get to know their strange ways. Try to keep them honest by going back to their origin, back to the field (when you can) to reflect on whatever messy reality is *necessarily* squeezed into them. It has to be this way, so get used to it. Then check the next chapter for a counterbalance to some of this scepticism.

Try this

Travelling from London to Leeds a few years back, mid-general election, I came across a crisp company seeking publicity by giving out packs adorned with party leaders' faces. It was almost an opinion poll: pick the party-pack you like.

What's the data backstory?

Note the Lib Dem crisps (yellow/orange) going like hot cakes, not a packet to be seen in the bin; Conservative (blue) not doing too badly, just visible over the rim; Labour (red), piled high, unwanted.

... or maybe not.

Think about what you see here, reflect on the gritty practicalities and anything in this image that could be relevant and give ten reasons (yes, ten – serious or daft) why the number of crisp packets in the bins is what it is. There are no correct answers – this is a game – but you'll find some suggestions at the end of the chapter. If we simply gave you the data, you might almost be tempted to swallow it; with a picture, you see the life behind the data. That's the skill: to picture that life.

Jargon

- *Data*: from Latin, meaning 'that which is given' – except never forget it really isn't given, it's partly made. The hazard is there from the start.

Crisps, a few explanations

- People choose flavour, not political party.

- They're all the same flavour (true actually), but people *think* they're different.

- It's all to do with the direction most people walk past the bins at this time of day.

- It's due to the kind of folk who live around King's Cross railway station.

- It's rush hour, so it's the sort who commute by train.

- The Lib Dem guy has the best patter.

- People fancy him.

- Labour voters like crisps less than other voters do.

- The Lib Dem guy is a crisp glutton and eats them himself.

- He's a party sympathizer giving out two at once.

- There's a snarling dog out of shot on the Lab side of the picture.

- Labour voters are boycotting the crisp company.

- Con voters resent surveys, but love crisps, and finish up in the middle.

- The Lib Dems heard about it and bussed in a load of supporters to swing the result.

- It's mostly kids who ignore politics but like yellow.

- The Labour guy is sneezing everywhere – avoid.

- The Labour bin has just been refilled and so the quantity in the bin at any one time doesn't tell you anything (the difference between counting stock and flow – note the boxes at the back).

- That other guy has been standing in the way of the Labour bin all day, arguing politics.

- This really is a fair snapshot of the state of political opinion – at that time.

- People are not taking the crisps, they're putting them back (the weirdest explanation anyone ever suggested to me, but points for imagination).

- Some combination of any of the above. Etc.

Intense seeing. Engraving of the brig *Vigilante* by
J. Hawksworth, from an anti-slavery pamphlet for the
Religious Society of Friends in London, 1822.

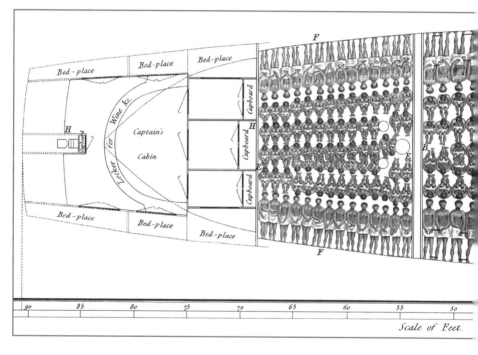

4

But count in human

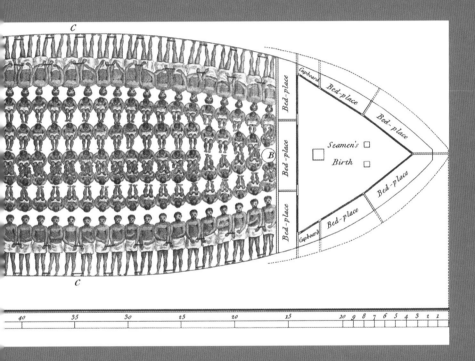

Context, every time

Between ten and fifteen million slaves were shipped across the Atlantic. Maybe two million died on the crossing.[1] These numbers are hard to imagine. The picture helps vivify them – and it's harrowing. What unhinges you is the practical detail, the way it begins with calm, draughtsman-like precision to restore life and context to those unimaginable numbers; how each human figure is distinct, each life observed – but packed like one soulless cargo. Maybe we notice the scale across the bottom of the picture and look up to see what five airless feet means for three or four adult men or maybe five women; or how people are sorted by size and kind, women huddled together, all to show us the merciless efficiency of this trade – and tell us we are in hell.

Edward Tufte, a data-visualization guru, uses this picture as an example of what he calls 'serious seeing'. He says the exactness, the detail, the quantification are moral; each life witnessed, then shown wretched in this space, 'a portrait of individual suffering multiplied by 347 people and then millions'. If, when we think of numbers, measurement and the rest of those quantifying tools we use to try to reach for the truth, one picture can remind us to keep the numbers alive, to show us what they can truly show in a human context, I choose this one.[2]

Two crude, exaggerated attitudes to numbers:

1. They're objective, revelatory, truth-seeking. The data don't lie! Seize the power of data!

2. They're lies and damned lies, they strut their pious claims to objectivity, but we know they're flaky, selective, at it – like the shadowy forces who abuse them.

In the naivety or overconfidence of 1 – look, data! – you can easily be fooled. In the disillusion of 2 – it's all lies! – you flounce off to the safety of old prejudices, refusing to believe anything ever again that isn't already barricaded in your cynical heart.

Not many are that far gone in either direction. But we're all tempted to quick judgements. If it's a number we like, we're eager to think it a 1, objective and true; if it's a number we don't like, it'll be a 2, most likely dodgy. The trouble with both is that they treat numbers like they're black or white, right or wrong, we can accept some and reject others, and we know which.

There is an alternative, obviously – a middle way between the naivety of 1 and the cynicism of 2. But the bad news is predictable: the middle way takes work. It means that all numbers need interpretation, all of them. They do not speak for themselves.[3]

To a lot of people, that's a drag. Learning to interpret numbers can take a lifetime – the books describe dozens of skills and then, just when you think you're on your way to grasping a few, the best of the books comes along to say it's an art.[4] Must we? What can be said in the few pages we have left to talk about numbers, before moving on to all the other smart-thinking crying out for attention?

First, breathe... and... relax. Interpreting numbers might take a little work, but often only a little. Humanize them, put them into a living context and we're halfway there. This requires almost no technical skill. Context-giving is a big thing in smart-thinking.

Here's a simple way of stating the problem, from Tom and Dave Chivers.[5] The number 2 means what, exactly? In daily life, without context, nothing, as we've said before. Two what? Two shotgun blasts to the head, or a £2 annual pay rise? Big, small, serious or not, context is meaning.

Easy, in principle. So let's try some harder tests: is £1 million a big number? To you and me, probably; to the economy as a whole? Peanuts. So it depends... on context. How about £1 billion? Still depends. Added to the NHS budget over five years, it's up less than 0.2 per cent a year, far lower than inflation.[6] So maybe it's big. Maybe not. Is thirty-seven people dying bad? Might be. Depends how, over what period, compared with what, in answer to what question. Is 'up 20 per cent' a lot? Dunno; 20 per cent of next to nothing is still next to nothing; 20 per cent of a lot could be a big deal. What if a risk doubles? Depends what it was to start with. And so on.

All straightforward – but can't be stressed enough. The only reason it's necessary to say all this is that numbers have a bizarre habit of drifting into abstraction, context-free, almost as if we've forgotten that the reason we use them is to count something that matters to us. So we see 'up 30 per cent' and decide it's a big deal, without knowing what it was to start with, and so with little idea how much 30 per cent matters. Millions and billions can likewise sound like big news, full of fury, with all those intimidating zeros on the end.

Either that or we go the other way and just switch off, finding these numbers so remote and abstract that we stop paying attention because we can't make sense of them. Either way, this is information that fails to inform, as people struggle to calibrate or imagine what the claims mean on the ground.

But there is a partial antidote to this numberwang, and it's context, which locates numbers in our world, the human world. Quite simply, it's what brings them to life, and once they are alive and less abstract, we can make better sense of them. This can be easier than it sounds because you're already alive and human, allegedly, and know what a human context means. You already carry that map.

In fact, 'mapping' is not a bad metaphor.[7] Work out where to place a number on our map – the map of our own lives – and we begin to see what it's worth.

How do we do this in practice? One of the best ways is with the most simple, naive questions: 'And is that a *big* number?' Naive maybe, but powerful. I made half a career from asking that question, and plenty of important people looked silly trying to answer it.[8]

Here's £10 million for school singing lessons, says a government minister, riding the wave of a popular TV show about choirs. And is that a big number? Context: there are about ten million school kids. What's that when it's mapped? It's £1 each a year, or £30 for a teacher for one class a year, if you're lucky.

And that's your £10 million, mapped to the classroom. Even big economic numbers can be brought home if we divide them between the humans they're meant to affect.

For a different kind of mapping, take an abstraction that's initially all but impossible to make sense of, which seems to scream: 'big!', 'bad!' and 'danger!' but again lacks human proportion. See below.

> Big, scary fact: burnt toast contains a nasty called acrylamide, which... causes cancer! Footnote to big, scary fact: possibly, though still unlikely, if you eat about 160 slices every day. NB: do not do this. 'I could burst' has been known (mind you, stomach rupture, if fatal, sure cuts the risk of cancer).
>
> The UK Food Standards Agency was launching a public scare information campaign about acrylamide in burnt toast, called 'Go for Gold!', until my colleagues at the Winton Centre put the numbers in context – in this case, pointing out how much toast it would probably take – to help map the risk onto any plausible breakfast. After which the FSA softened the campaign. Good for them. But what were they thinking? I think they were thinking without human proportion, relying instead on categories of risky or safe, good or bad. Fixed categories are tempting, not always useful. They're what make 'scary' so easy to assert, as it's all scary if you skip human proportion. Even breathing oxygen and drinking water – see hyponatraemia – can cause harm at the wrong dose. Sleeping with someone exposes you to radiation; a long kiss to another potential carcinogen. That is, life tends to be messier than our abstract, two-way division between

A good statistic is one that aids a decision or shapes an opinion. For a stat to do either of those, it must be dragged within the everyday. That's your job – to do the dragging.

Chip Heath and Dan Heath, *Made to Stick*

Risk, toasted.

> *darkness and light, safe and not, etc. To interpret*
> *numbers properly, we need to get down to earth where*
> *they're lived.*

Since context and proportion are often easy, anyone who doesn't supply them makes me twitchy. If a risk or scare (or benefit) doesn't have proper, human proportion, be sceptical. So I chose the most grounded, homely thing I could think of for our next pic about numbers, as a reminder to look for human context whenever possible. Here it is: an absurdity of toast.

Toast is as everyday as it comes, real, tangible – you can eat it for breakfast and you know two slices from 160. Let's see the percentages and relative risks by all means, but let's also watch these abstractions and demand the absolute, real toast, too. Show us how many slices – and make 'count the toast' the metaphorical antidote to abstraction and big words or numbers.[9] 'The end is nigh', yeah, yeah, but show me the toast. 'We will transform, revolutionize, turbo-charge the future...', right, but let's see the toast – the quantitative equivalent of 'smell the coffee'.

'Mapping' is an Edward Tufte metaphor. It's what the picture of the slave ship does, he says: maps the raw, unimaginable fifteen million so that you can almost feel it. As ever, mapping is imperfect and not always straightforward, but it's a first step. Once mapped to the human lot, numbers are often easier to interpret.

Another phrase for what we're after here is 'ground truth'. It doesn't mean the definitive, absolute truth, but the metric of the kitchen, the neighbourhood, the home, the school, the business, the human dimension, the ground that we people stand on, as opposed to the view from 30,000 feet or the world of abstraction. 'What's that when it's at home?' goes a good down-to-earth question. It's easier to think about almost anything quantified if the numbers are in reach of ordinary experience on a human scale. Then we see what kind of sense they make, if any.

> *Binge-watching TV can kill you, says the news. Well, sure, there's a risk of pulmonary embolism if you sit around a lot, but let's map the risk onto an evening on the sofa. According to the research, even if the risk was true and causal, on average for one pulmonary embolism we'd have to watch more than five hours a night for 12,000 years.*
>
> *That example makes the problem sound easy. It can be, except... sometimes the numbers look like they're the toast when they're not. Over twenty-five years in London, 361 cyclists were killed, say David and Tom Chivers in* How to Read Numbers. *A lot? Too many, for sure. But although in one way that number is surely human, it's not easy to map 361 deaths to my next ride. A number can be true, but not useful. What I really want to know is the risk to me, now – which, say Tom and David, is one in ten million, a probability. So in this case the 361 deaths sound more immediate, but they're the abstraction, they're not mapped, not grounded, lacking context, just fourteen per year bundled up out of who knows how many rides, to make the threat look as big as possible. For me in this case it's an abstract probability that's the toast, the one in ten million. It can be useful to think of context as answering the question 'What's this number for, how do I use it?'*

Almost anything, left vague enough, can sound like a big deal, but how big exactly? Take expert punditry, especially forecasting – which is superb at sounding big while saying nothing. 'There's a real possibility of economic headwinds because of what's happening in the Gulf.' Yep, usually is. But 'real possibility'? What the (insert expletive) does 'real possibility' mean? All it really means – as Dan Gardner, who writes on risk and futurology puts it – is that it won't disobey the laws of physics.

'Vague verbiage forecasting,' Dan Gardner and Philip Tetlock call this (*Superforecasting*). A phrase I like is 'knowledge theatre' – the show of substance when the set's cardboard. In the corporate world you can pay a lot of money for this show. Instead, show me your toast, quantify your 'real possibility' and your deadly acrylamide, else you're just waving your arms. If the numbers truly matter, show us how.

> *I had a call from the BBC. 'We're thinking about how to make stories about refugees from the Syrian civil war hit home,' the producer said. The numbers, vast as they were, seemed to have lost meaning. Was the audience numb? So, for a short radio piece to try to hit home for a UK audience... we brought the Syrian numbers home to the UK. Here's what I said:*
>
> *'Say you're one of the two and a half million people who live in the huge conurbation of Greater Manchester. And then you leave. All of you. [Long pause] Followed by Tyne and Wear, exiting the UK as if life depends on it. On your heels comes Merseyside, the entire population. After that, Glasgow, all of it. Then about half the population of Greater London.*

'If you're Syria, that's a scaled equivalent of the refugees reported by the UN to be fleeing the country. Where do you go? Many Syrians go to Lebanon, a country so small that immigration has swollen its population by getting on for 40 per cent. Forty per cent growth is about 100 years' worth of the latest net migration to the UK. So you'd be welcome, of course.

'And those are just refugees heading to other countries. There are millions more displaced within Syria itself. For a UK equivalent, add to our earlier total: the rest of Greater London, Birmingham, Belfast, every person in Cornwall, Devon, Dorset, Somerset, all of Norfolk, Suffolk, plus the entire remaining population of Scotland, the entire population of Wales, and then throw in Sheffield, Bristol, Brighton, Swindon, Plymouth, Coventry, Leicester, Leeds, Cambridge...'

And so on... The UK is bigger than Syria, which is why we called this a scaled equivalent – a reminder that mapping means making judgements. Listeners found it striking. The BBC repeated it. It wasn't the definitive way of thinking about the war, just a rough and partial answer to one question – 'What might carnage on that scale be like?' – by bringing the numbers home.

If the biggest problem with numbers is what the thing counted is (see the previous chapter), the next is this: the size without size, the number theatre without context, the abstractions that are off the map.

But, but, but... in a world obsessed with counting, and with the bottom line especially, does the advice to 'count the toast' reduce everything to money?

Whoa! Who mentioned money? A slice of toast is worth practically nothing. Its point is only that we already know our way around toast. It's the familiarity.

Another but... 'I hate numbers, they're inhuman.' Well, they can be. That's what we're trying to fight against. And we keep trying because, used well, numbers can be good for people; they're recognition: if you're counted, this says your life and experience count.

And that's us mostly done with numbers (there's a smidgen more, especially if you count the chapter on chance). Most of the pop-bookery about them consists of variations on the ideas in the last two chapters, definition and contextualized proportion. But those variations are weasels of cunning and discovery.[10]

Not so fast...

The slave ship is a harrowing, astonishing example of how numbers can be contextualized and humanized, even to help show the depths of inhumanity. But how often does context-giving work so well? One reason it succeeds here is because the facts themselves are morally clear. But what if the human context is itself messy? Then invoking it won't clarify the numbers for you.

In other words, these context-giving techniques can be invaluable, but let's not kid ourselves: a lot of evidence is messy, hard to classify, harder to interpret, because the life it describes is messy, and so is the context. Sometimes we need numbers of every kind, including abstractions like averages, to grasp even a fraction of what's up, because what's up is itself complicated. Sometimes averages and probabilities can be the most useful evidence we have (about risks, for example), even though in one way these are the most abstract numbers of all, about no individual in existence. Some economic numbers (national debt, for instance) have no homely equivalent; they are not like household budgets (because nations don't die or retire, and never have to pay off their debts entirely), so you can't simply map the numbers for national debt to a household to provide context – though journalists and politicians have been known to try. Worse, the most emotionally engaging numbers can be the most deceptive, so we can't confer 'ground truth' on a number simply because it touches the heart. In other words, the problem with the idea of context is: 'How do I know which is the right context?'

We can look at numbers from many angles – and arguments about numbers are often exactly that, a fight over which angle or context matters most. Deaths from Covid-19, for example, can be viewed as years lost by each victim (which looked terrible, typically about ten years each on average). Is that the right context? Sounds human to me. Or they can be seen in the context of the fall in average life expectancy for the population – from about eighty to seventy-nine for men in the UK, and from eighty-four to eighty-three for women – which doesn't seem so bad, especially if you add the context that this is where the UK was about ten years earlier. Which context is right? Which is the toast?

Let's step back and remember those dragonfly eyes (see page 28). Interpretation means coming at evidence in different ways, using one technique to check another, all the time aware of the limitations. So, as in this chapter, sense-check the stats by putting them in a humanizing context or by comparing them with personal stories. But also do the opposite, and test emotionally resonant stories with the stats, to check that a story is more than a one-off. Both are contextualizing, but in different ways. Use stories and experience to test numbers; use numbers to test stories and experience. Use principles to remind us why we're counting; use the evidence from counting to challenge or vivify principles. Use one framing of the numbers to test another, and to help you work out what it is you really want to know. In short, use contexts, maps, techniques (plural).

If all that makes life tricky when you crave simplicity, maybe ask if your craving is helping. But also remember the slave ship. Numbers in the right context can sometimes bring experience and data together to be compelling. So put it above your desk as an idealization of contextualization — and then remember how hard it can be to realize ideals.

Try this

Almost a repeat of the crisps, but this time the number is explicit. Take this piece of counting:

'Wow! A bloke just ate twelve sausages.'

Then, like the crisps, take a minute to ask a few questions, to fish for the practical context that reveals why twelve could be no big deal. I saw this somewhere years ago – sorry for forgetting where. Answers serious or daft. Some suggestions:

- How big were the sausages? (tiny, cocktail sausages)
- How big was he? (vast)

- When did he last eat? (he'd starved in the desert for weeks)

- Over what period did he eat twelve sausages? (one of those three-day wedding feasts)

- Did he finish every sausage? (no, nibbled them)

- Was he a professional sausage-taster? (yes, spat them out)

- Was this the South Idaho primary of the All-America Sausage-Eating Competition? (yep, lowest competitive total ever)

- Did anyone see him eat the sausages, or was it self-reported? (he's always saying this stuff)

- Or what if he really did eat twelve huge sausages super-fast? (he did, couldn't believe it, hope he's OK.)

Spirit of Nessie. The Loch Ness Monster seen on holiday over Greece.

5

Beware nature's fake news

Chance *will* fool you

Saw Nessie, the Loch Ness Monster, once. Looked vaguely like her at least. Then she vanished. But for a moment it was nice to believe, in an unbelieving way.

Did it mean anything? Do I have to answer that? OK, no. It was just nature's fake news.

Now there's a provocative phrase. Been wondering whether to give it life and I'm still unsure. The downside is obvious: 'fake news' is a notorious insult with dodgy associations. Do we really want to go there? Then again, that's what makes it kinda catchy. Though there's a little more to this than notoriety, I hope.

So what does it mean: 'nature's fake news'? How can nature, of all things, be fake?

Easily. By showing us beasts in the clouds is one way, or anything that sort of looks like something else, but isn't. Happens all the time, as you know. Maybe you've seen the Jesus-on-toast phenomenon (next pic).

To be clear (because you have to be, on this), I'm not calling Jesus fake. I just doubt it's him on the toast. More likely, given all the slices in all the toasters in all the world, now and then one pops up face-like, by chance, assuming – sometimes generously – that no human got creative with the matches.

As these 'pictures' are often sketchy – note the moustache consuming the right nostril, here – I go with those who think the real God could do better, if he intended a likeness. And why toast for a canvas? Haven't you seen his sunsets? If you want evidence for God, in this case I wouldn't count the toast.

Anyway, my brother says it looks more like Lemmy from the rock band Motörhead.

Looks a bit like... but is it?

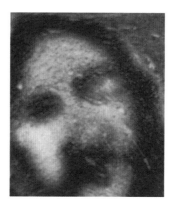

Or is it...?

Or neither?

So maybe God likes a joke. Alternatively, you get the idea: chance, or randomness, does not always look how we expect chance to look – like a mess, like chaos, or like nothing at all. Sometimes it looks like Lemmy. But mess is often how we characterize it, a characterization you hear in the word 'noise', for example, used to mean chance or meaningless data, which emphasizes its total uselessness, shapelessness and annoyance. But the problem with 'noise' as a metaphor is it gives the impression that chance data will look or sound like pandemonium. The crucial point about 'noise' is how much it can sound like your favourite tune. So don't look for noise expecting to see (or hear) noise. Look for the sound or appearance of meaning, listen for a tune, then remember... this too could be noise. That's why I say it might not be so ridiculous to talk about nature's fake news, because it emphasizes how much this can look like the real thing, and that's the point – appearances can deceive, and chance is the great deceiver.

After three decades of mulling this over from time to time, I've come to suspect it's bad intuition for what chance looks like that causes its power to be so underestimated. We think we know how to spot it – 'Yeah, yeah, we know all about chance' is a reaction I hear often – but we're looking for the wrong thing. We look for what's most obvious – the clear fluke – when we should be alert to what's most treacherous: our belief that we've seen real meaning.

More serious than cloud-spotting – because we're coming to the point now – patterns in information are also ubiquitous. And the same kind of cloud-in-the-sky-looks-like-something-but-isn't-because-it's-just-randomness pops up time and again in these patterns, too. That is, it happens in data, and

in research, and in numbers, and in what we see and experience first-hand; in fact in evidence of all kinds, just about
everywhere, prolifically. Not once-in-a-while and weirdly, but
normally; chance stuff that merely looks significant; 'proof' that
seems to arise naturally, innocently, convincingly, about what
the world appears to be doing, but turns out to tell us sod-all –
and not because anyone's lying. They were simply duped when
it turned up on the toast, the data, the chart, as part of their
'lived experience', by chance, wherever, whatever, looking like it
meant something.

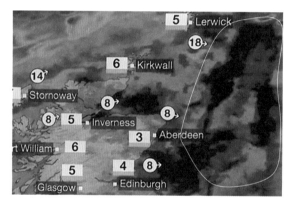

*Life's single lesson: that
there is more accident
to it than a man can
ever admit to in a
lifetime and stay sane.*

Thomas Pynchon

While we're on rock stars... A BBC weather forecast featuring Prince on guitar in the North Sea.
See him?

That's why I love these pictures: they link what everyone
knows, from seeing patterns in the sky, with the dangers in
seeing meaning in even apparently smart or direct evidence.
So feel the sense of recognition when you look at the patterns
in these pictures – and learn from the fact that they're not
what they seem.

If chance can arrange enough stuff to make it look like Prince is playing guitar in the weather off Aberdeen, it can easily produce a few random bits of data or experience to mess up our conclusions – unless we're on guard. A lot of people think they're on guard and do mathematical tests to convince themselves, tests that – guess what? – are also vulnerable to chance. As the writer and philosopher Robert Pirsig said:

> The real purpose of scientific method is to make sure Nature hasn't misled you into thinking you know something you don't actually know. There's not a mechanic or scientist or technician alive who hasn't suffered from that one so much that he's not instinctively on guard. That's the main reason why so much scientific and mechanical information sounds so dull and so cautious. If you get careless or go romanticizing scientific information, give it a flourish here and there, Nature will soon make a complete fool out of you. It does it often enough anyway even when you don't give it opportunities.[1]

You mean this kind of thing happens in science?

All the time.

What, convincingly, but just by chance?

All the time.

And clever people are fooled?

Yes.

By the science equivalent of Jesus on toast or beasts in clouds?

You got it. And in think-tanks, governments, business, the news, artificial intelligence... and us in our daily lives, when we try to learn from experience.

OK, show me how, chance guy...

> *Scan people's brains, compare what we see with their behaviour or mental health, and we can link behaviour to brain structure, yes? If a brain looks like this, it means people behave like that. It's called a brain-wide association study, and over the years we have found many exciting links between brain structure and behaviour.*
>
> *Or... thought we did. Then in March 2022 research showed that you could take two groups of twenty-five people – a typical study size – and come to opposite conclusions about the brain structure–behaviour correlation. In other words, there's so much noise/chance in the results, so much natural variation in people's scans, that the findings were akin to reading meaning into clouds in the brain. 'Vast swathes of published neuroimaging studies are spurious,' said one leading researcher. To be more reliable, studies need samples not of twenty-five, but thousands – a practical nightmare. If neuroimaging couldn't tell chance from meaning, maybe the task is not such a no-brainer. Never underestimate your chance of being fooled by chance.*

So how do we tell if nature's news is real and meaningful or fake/just chance? Delighted you asked. Really good question. Hard to answer. I've heard it said that almost the only question in statistics is 'What's the source/cause of the variation?' That is, what's making this thing change/go up and down? Is it chance or is it something else? What, exactly?

Begin with this thought: sorting chance from meaning can be one of the most intellectually fiendish tasks in all science, and all evidence. So start by showing the problem some respect.

Here's another example that's part science (public health), part news. In this case, the simple ups and downs in the data were given a meaning that probably wasn't there. They might have guessed this, simply by looking back at what the old chance ups and downs were typically like, but hey-ho...

This is a girl-meets-boy story (both straight). The boy has romantic notions about commitment. He believes in The Relationship. The girl has, let's say, a more mechanical interest: sex. Or maybe the other way round. Anyhow, there's an argument about whether young people should be taught only the mechanics of sex, contraception, etc., or also about relationships: that is, try to be in a stable one before you have a kid. Or should we keep morality out of it?

Let's take our story to the island of Orkney in Scotland a few years back, which had one of the worst rates of teen pregnancy in the developed world. OK, they said in Orkney, what can we do? Let's teach the value of relationships! What happened? Teen pregnancies halved. Halved! A drop that big couldn't be chance. The BBC duly gave it the 'wow!' treatment.

But what happened next? The number went straight back up again the following year (despite still teaching relationships). Cue puzzled faces.

Here's the thing: women do not line up to get knocked-up at an orderly rate. No, believe it or not, pregnancy numbers go up and down. And like a lot that goes up and down, it can mean nothing at all. A down can be nature's fake news. An up can be a chance blip. Or maybe it goes up and down for some other reason you didn't see. Maybe all the young men left the island to live on Shetland. Maybe one man left the island – you know the one.

Basically, stuff goes up and down anyway, for all sorts of reasons, some of them pure chance. Even if there's an underlying reason for a long-term up, it will likely go up and down on the way. This should be fantastically obvious. But chance ups and downs are hard to resist if they appear to serve your argument. While they might look meaningful, we must work harder to decide if they are. Oh, and Orkney is tiny, so it doesn't take many pregnancies to halve the teen pregnancy rate. Easy prey for chance.[2]

I found a headline a while back:

12 Things Currently Being Sold On eBay Because They Kinda Look Like Jesus

Let's adapt it:

Reported in a scientific journal

12 Things Currently Being Sold On eBay Because They Kinda Look Like Jesus

a 'Finding'

No kidding. Science has plenty of fakes – natural and human – mistaken for the real thing. Estimates of how much published science is doubtful are controversial and vary according to discipline, but it's often said to be a sizeable fraction, and a misreading of chance is often to blame. And if science struggles, imagine the junk elsewhere. Again, don't conclude all science is bad and turn cynic. There's a ton of good, too. But the difference between good and bad often begins with respect for the awesome versatility of chance.

Another testing example, winced over with a friend a while back: what if a celeb (worst case, David Attenborough) had a Covid jab, then a heart attack? Even if the jab was 100 per cent guaranteed safe, there'd be trouble – maybe we'd have to prop him up in a bush like he was still filming, lest people put 2 + 2 together in a flash of intuitive pattern-spotting to make 5 and reject the vaccine, even though this story would bring us no news about it. As far as the vaccine goes, it was nature's fake news.

The good news is you have an astonishing ability to discern patterns and give them meaning... it's a dog.

The bad news is you have an astonishing ability to discern patterns and give them meaning... it's not a hedgehog (it's a murmuration).[3]

It's because our knack for seeing meaning is so fast that we need a quick way to slow down. 'Nature's fake news' is one of those: a quick phrase, a red traffic light. It says stop and think, that's all. The danger is that we use this phrase to give the red light to any evidence we don't like the look of, as people do when shouting 'fake news' at each other. So once again, use 'nature's fake news' to question your own evidence first, evidence from others maybe later. It is not an insult, it's not to win an argument, it's to help us by asking if one possibility here is that there's no meaning at all, and to remind us that chance – however well we think we know it – has a genius for disguise. And, by the way, the more amazing the data, the more likely that chance is the explanation.

> *I have a badly chalked map of the UK and Ireland on green felt about two metres long, and a tub of dried macaroni: stick with me. Then in talks, when we get onto clusters – like a cancer cluster with many cases in one place, when people feel anxious about what it means and what caused it – I unfurl the map and ask what'll happen if we chuck the tubful of macaroni into the air. Where will it land, what patterns will it make – by chance?*

Sure enough, it clusters. And then you start... 'Oh, wow, look at Merseyside/Manchester. What's going on? And have you seen around Bristol (or did I stick those pieces together)? And then East Anglia, almost case-free. Weird, huh? What's in the water?' NB: I cleared the sea, but seem to have missed the west of Eire and Northern Ireland (I stood near Hull).

We see clusters as a clue that something's up. They're also the normal stuff of chance. Life clusters. Just does. What did you expect: the macaroni would fall evenly spaced – is that what you think chance means? So do clusters ever mean anything? Occasionally yes, emphatically. There can be meaning, and there can be no meaning at all.

PS: Say this with care. People don't like hearing that their cluster is chance. They might think you don't care, or mean there's no explanation for their cancer, or even that their illness is fake. It's none of this. All it means is that chance brings all the real cases to one place. Assume that a cluster means one cause for all – 'Look, a phone mast nearby!' – and you might miss the true causes (plural).

I know, this is not really nature faking anything; it's us, being credulous. But you can think of it either way: the fooled or the fooler. All we're trying to do with these metaphors is slow the rage for quick conclusions, and remind ourselves not to trust too soon what seems self-evident or natural, or smart.[4]

Not so fast

Things that look like news can be nature's fakes. But sometimes it's the other way round: things that look like nothing can be the main event. Maybe something starts small, seems inconsequential, but changes the world. Maybe it looks like chance, but that chance event is devastating. It's possible to see both meaning where there is none, and nothing where there's meaning. So don't be too trigger-happy about dismissing things.

Inevitably no simple rule can steer between the two risks of seeing what isn't there and missing what is (well, people use simple rules, but often they're not up to it). Start by using your dragonfly eyes and learning to be sensitive to how we're fooled both ways. Then, for a variety of real meaning that's easily missed or dismissed, see the next chapter.

Try this

Someone writes to you predicting the winner of a football match. They're right. They write again the next week and they're right again. And the next. And the next. And the next. Then they ask you for £1,000 to name the winner of next week's game. Either they're psychic or a brilliant forecaster. How do they do it, using nothing more than chance?

Jargon

- *Apophenia*: seeing patterns of any kind where they might not exist, including in data. The more complex your data, the easier to find a fake pattern.

- *Type 1 error* and *false positives*: both mean that your experiment or analysis saw something when there was nothing real to see, maybe mistaking chance for meaning. As ever, there's an opposite risk, *the type 2 error* or *false negative*: missing something real that was there all along (see the next chapter).

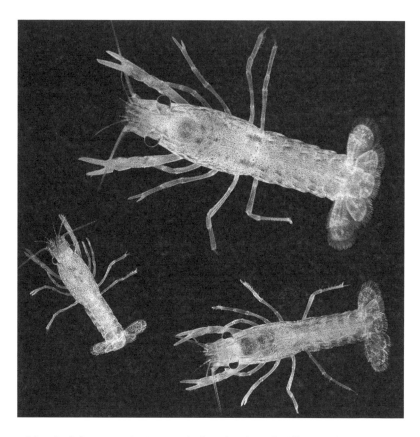

Identical, but not. G. Vogt et al., 'Production of Different Phenotypes from the Same Genotype in the Same Environment by Developmental Variation', *Journal of Experimental Biology*, vol. 211, 2008.

6

But treasure
the funnies

Order tells you something;
so does disorder

The most telling moment in science? For Isaac Asimov, it was when someone said: 'That's funny.'[1]

Here's a funny...

In mid-1990s Germany aquarium enthusiasts noticed that one of their species of crayfish had no males, ever, generation after generation. 'That's funny,' they said. Scientists agreed.

It turned out that the females had started cloning themselves, in an aquarium, beginning with one spontaneous mutation in one mother – let's call her Eve – for a whole new species never seen in the wild, all female, just like that, in a fish tank. Amazing.

I tell this story in my book *The Hidden Half*. It gets funnier. Those scientists realized they could use Eve's new brood to investigate the age-old nature–nurture or gene–environment question. Because if these creatures are clones, you'd expect them to be pretty similar, right? And if they do turn out differently, it must be the environment, right? What else is there if the genes are identical? So researchers put their new species – a crayfish they named Marmorkrebs – into tanks in a lab to study.

But they went further and standardized the environment too, as far as humanly possible, right down to the same person examining the Marmorkrebs on every occasion using the same variety of gloves. So, same genes, same environment, same everything. How did their Marmorkrebs turn out?

Chalk and cheese. Seriously. The differences were astonishing. In one batch, one Marmorkrebs was twenty times the weight of another. Twenty! They differed physically and behaviourally: some gregarious, some loners, some bossy, some meek. Lifespan varied hugely. So did egg-laying, feeding and sleeping habits. The differences, often pronounced, went on and on. The picture shows cloned Marmorkrebs from the same batch of eggs hatched at the same time and growing in identical environments, with the size differences screaming out. Why so unalike, when *everything* was the same?

This was funny on stilts – and hugely awkward for the standard story of genes and environment. Even combined, these two forces are evidently not everything; at least not the way we usually see them. We argue over which makes people differ most: genes or environment? You're probably more in one camp than the other yourself. But what if, often, the answer is neither? What if it can be something else altogether, some weird third thing never thought of? And not in a trivial, borderline way, but as a game-changing influence? All those old nature–nurture arguments wouldn't become useless exactly, but they'd sure need revision. This is the reason 'funny' matters: it hints that something's up, and maybe this something can shake a whole intellectual order – if only we'd let it. 'Treasure your exceptions,' said an early geneticist, William Bateson, 100 years ago. Treasure the funnies.

Problem is, let's face it, not many of us like having our intellectual order shaken, as you can tell by the fact that most of us had never heard of the Marmorkrebs, or other cloned creatures like them. Whatever's going on here should figure heavily when we talk about what makes living things (including us) turn out how they do.[2] Instead, even the fact that massive, untraceable variation like this exists is largely unknown, and the story of the Marmorkrebs made little impact outside a few specialist journals. All we do is scrap over one order or another, genes v. environment. This other thing (whatever it is) doesn't get a look-in.

Why not? Maybe because it doesn't fit, it's irregular, disorderly, unpredictable. It messes up our categories – those again – and spoils the comfort of a familiar flaming row. So we're not sure we want to know all this, because it might mean work and uncertainty. We've built such expectations, such convictions about how things work, tried so hard to make the world neat, that we scarcely know what to think when the evidence drops a plate.[3]

In the research world, the randomness revealed by the Marmorkrebs and others has been named 'the gloomy prospect' – gloomy because it makes the scientist's dream of orderly explanation that bit more elusive.[4] 'Gloomy prospect' is quite the giveaway. It suggests no one wants to go there. Too bad. If you want to think seriously, you're going. Follow the disorder, not just the order; treasure the exceptions, the funnies, however much they threaten your ideas. Treasure them *because* they threaten your ideas.

That's 'funny' for you: the first realization your existing order might not be right, a hint of what could be paradigm-shifting. Gary Klein's book on insight, *Seeing What Others Don't*, says that insights big and small often come from zooming in when something's funny.[5]

Trouble is – you knew this was coming – how to react to funnies isn't always clear. Sometimes funny is merely weird, a fluke, outlier data caused by the kind of chance we can ignore because it's essentially meaningless, like a face in the clouds (see everything in the previous chapter).

At other times, unusual evidence is a sign of something big, a hint that the world just doesn't work the way we thought it did, when maybe we're picking up something fundamental. For my money, it's here – interpreting 'funny' in the border-line cases between order and disorder, chance and meaning – that knowing stuff is most teasing and fascinating, and the techniques of smart-thinking are stretched to their limits and beyond. It could be fundamental, it could be nothing. Tricky, eh?

On the one hand, we have evidence like the Marmorkrebs (I love these crayfish for being so obliviously troublemaking) – a reminder of how totally our sense of order can ignore scream-ing exceptions. So don't demand too much order.

On the other hand, order is what knowledge is, so of course we want more. Regularities suggest some underlying truth that's more than chaos. Marcus du Sautoy's book *Thinking Better* makes a compelling case for pattern-spotting as our greatest intellectual gift, talking of it as a supreme mental shortcut (see Chapter 9) – and what's pattern-spotting if not a sense for order and regularity?[6] So we should treasure our reg-ularities, too. But can we do that without missing the funnies? It's another fine art, judging between seeing too much and seeing too little.

It was writing *The Hidden Half* and learning about the Marmorkrebs that gave me one of the pictures for this book (see above), because I suggested that every researcher should stick it above the desk as a reminder of all the enigmatic vari-ables that could screw up their search for order.[7] Here's another way of thinking about the power of funnies...

In The Black Swan *in 2007 Nassim Taleb made waves in the world of smart-thinking when he described a big idea via a single metaphor... the black swan.*

For a long time Europeans said there was no such thing; it was a byword for impossibility. Then they turned up in Australia, thus becoming a neat metaphor for the unlikely or exceptional, which Nassim latched onto. But his really big claim was that it's Black Swans (note his capital letters) that shape life; not the everyday order, but the funnies, the disorder, the shake-up caused by rare events.

The global financial crash of 2008 was all the endorsement his ideas would need – a catastrophic event thought ridiculously unlikely by many, which radically changed our conception of how banking and the economy worked. His examples go far and wide, from new technologies to political movements.

He defines a Black Swan first as an outlier, as it lies outside regular expectations. Nothing in the past can convincingly point to it. Second, it has extreme impact. Third, despite being an outlier, we concoct explanations after the fact as if it should have been predictable.

A few Black Swans explain 'almost everything in our world,' Nassim says, 'from the success of ideas and religions to the dynamics of historical events, to elements of our personal lives'. Hard to resist a picture, don't you think? The Black Swan, a vivid, well-fitting metaphor for the exceptions to our belief that we've nailed life's patterns. If you've any acquaintance with the Black Swan, it'll be the most unoriginal picture in the book. But the idea has become so popular, how can we leave it out?[8]

Treasure your exceptions!... Keep them always uncovered and in sight. Exceptions are like the rough brickwork of a growing building which tells that there is more to come and shows where the next construction is to be.

William Bateson

All this is a pain. It's a whole other way of being wrong.

Let's step back for a moment and try to impose a crude typology on this wrongness. The first way of being wrong is the one often targeted by smart-thinking books:

1. We're dumb – cognitively biased, irrational, innumerate, herds of the like-minded, it's all in our heads, etc., etc.

But the second way of being wrong, revealed by the Marmorkrebs and the black swan, adds another layer that is frustration incarnate.

2. Stuff is *really* hard – no matter how smart our thinking. The world is inherently complicated, infernally difficult to predict and understand, so the problem of knowing what's up is not only in our heads, it's out there with a vengeance.

Here are Brian Christian and Tom Griffiths in *Algorithms to Live By* because the point stands repeating: 'Life is full of problems that are, quite simply, *hard*. And the mistakes made by people often say more about the intrinsic difficulties of the problem than about the fallibilities of human brains.'

Problems are *hard* not least because answers keep changing, the conceptual order we think we've nailed turns out wrong with such consequences – for good or ill – and not because we're biased or cognitively useless, but because causation can be a shifting heap of spaghetti as life and context evolve; and nailing spaghetti, well, good luck.

Or maybe causes and explanations that we overlook in the tangle are only revealed later, when we finally pull on one of those strands to discover it mattered. Until then, who knew...? Only a very few guessed the significance of shadow banking or the financial contracts that did so much harm to the financial system in the global financial crash. The world, as you might have noticed, is full of such surprises. As Nassim says, it's hard to see any upset coming, but when it does, it can shift paradigms. Sure, the dumbness of 1 – of all our cognitive limitations – is a problem. Tackle it, if we can. But the elusive outside world of 2 is every bit as awkward. In that world, if you think you know, just give it time. There could be a funny along in a moment.

I'll put up my hand: I'm mildly optimistic about the possibility of thinking tolerably well – 'There's a chance, is what I'm saying' – if we're organized, careful and humble; I'm more worried at how easily people become overconfident about what we can achieve in a world of hard problems, given nature's cunning, given her tendency to drop unexpected third factors or previous unknowns into our big paradigms. That's not to be down on us and our brains, and it's not being hope-less; it's respecting the complexity out there. If you accept only one authorial rant from *Thinking in Pictures*, make it that. In fact this is another of my beefs with smart-thinking: it puts too much of the problem inside our heads. If that's where you start, it's easy to conclude that we must all be a bit cognitively hopeless. But maybe, at least now and then, smart starts in the wrong place.

Not the solution to all your problems that you wanted. Sorry about that – though not that sorry, if I'm honest. As far as I'm concerned, that's how it is. But if the downside is that life is full of surprises, the upside is that life is full of surprises.

> *A funny helped win 2021's Nobel Prize for economics. The story begins with the laws (big word, 'laws', a major claim to order if ever there was) of supply and demand. Then there was a rise in the minimum wage in New Jersey, but not in neighbouring Pennsylvania where there were similar labour markets. Everything we knew about the laws of supply and demand said that if the price of labour (pay) went up – other things being equal – then demand (employers hiring workers) would go down; there'd be more unemployment. Joshua Angrist, one of the Nobel winners, showed that when the minimum wage went up in New Jersey compared with Pennsylvania, this didn't happen. In this case, the law wasn't a law.*
>
> *'Wait, what?' said a whole economics profession, some ridiculing the finding. But it wasn't easily dismissed. There's been huge effort since then to work out why the law's writ didn't run, and in what conditions this applies. The shock forced economics to change. Emphasis*

shifted to what they called 'natural experiments', when life offered up the kind of comparisons that could never be deliberately devised. You can't make New Jersey and Pennsylvania run separate minimum-wage policies but, if they do, you can study them: that's a natural experiment. Empirical evidence gained status, economic theory lost a little. 'Funnies' – exceptions to general laws and theories – carried more weight. They called this shift (and the phrase is telling) 'the credibility revolution'. They'd been shocked by a finding about labour markets, but were also shocked that such shocks could happen to them, so they changed how they worked and learned to treasure the funnies a little more.

Not so fast

Aren't you just growing to hate this 'on the one hand… on the other' schtick?

Treasure your regularities because they're knowledge, but don't hold on too fast. Treasure your irregularities (funnies), too, but not if they're meaningless scraps of chance.

Pay too much attention to every radical revisionist or claim of a shock finding and you'll end up feeling dizzy. So don't do that. But do be sure not to miss the surprising findings that matter.

'But how do I know which is which?' you scream. 'How do I know when the funnies matter and when they don't?' Order is knowledge, but too much order is false knowledge. Disorder could be knowledge, too, except when it isn't anything at all. Arrghhh!

All I can offer is the tough love that this is unsurprising, and we better get used to a world of 'buts' and 'maybes' and 'sometimes' and 'ifs' and 'watch out!' and borderline cases without simple rules. At least then we're better prepared to live with life's many surprises. And how is that? Sometimes (not always... arrghh!), by holding our truths lightly. Avoid nailing ourselves to them. Watch for exceptions and at least be willing to rethink, even if you decide later that this funny was a joke.

The dilemma is right there in how we should react to Nassim Taleb's argument that Black Swans – extreme events with low probabilities – can be massively influential. Because if he's right, how afraid should we be of extreme risks? Some people who read him presumably finish up highly sensitized. But it's hard to say if they're right, as there's also a risk we could overdo it, that out of fear of extremes we could take error-avoidance to an extreme. So, underreact, or overreact? Every thinking risk has a countervailing risk, with no easy way of knowing where you stand between them.[9]

Try this

Say there's a river with a one in a 100-year chance of flooding. Then it floods twice in seven years. Tell two stories. One, why this pattern is boringly consistent with expectations and everything we already know, based on probability (hold on to the regularity). And two, why it changes everything (treasure the irregularity). Then say how you can know which is true. Is it chance, or meaning?

Next, if you're still following this, decide what action you'd take (if any) if you were in charge around here, given these two floods in seven years. Then decide what you would do if you happened to live there. If there's a difference between you the policymaker and you the resident, explain it.

Jargon

- *Normalcy bias* (a bias again, sorry): wanting to stick with what you already know and understand; being tempted to disregard new and threatening information; sometimes a kind of inertia or state of denial. Though watch it, as one alternative is overreaction.

Don't miss it, by pgrizz.[1]

7

Focus, but don't

Seeing what
you're missing

Hey, like my gate?

Nice gate, huh? Solid, high, sound hinges, opens and closes like a gate should, strong latch, secure, suitably rustic, absolutely fit for purpose. Perfect for getting in and out. It's a perfect gate.

...

What?

...

Oh, that. Hmm, see what you mean. Does kinda change things, doesn't it? And frankly, in this case, it's easy to see the... er, initial assessment had a blind spot. What's missing is conspicuously not there.

'In life and business, the person with the fewest blind spots wins,' say Shane Parrish and co. in the very first line of the intro to *The Great Mental Models*. 'Removing blind spots means we see, interact with, and mover close to understanding reality.'

Right then, don't have blind spots, don't miss things. Sorted.

'Well, duh...' you say. That's not smart, it's crashingly obvious. As if we don't know not to miss things. In fact it's so obvious it's almost annoying. It's obvious advice, and what's missed is often obvious after the fact. So don't tell me I should have seen it. *Of course* I should've seen it. I know already. And as if the world blunders ahead, not looking left or right; as if 'So then, what are we missing?' isn't the final cliché of every big decision.

Smart-thinking can be like that when you distil it: not far off a banality, little different from a proverb. But that's what's intriguing about this branch of smart-thinking: why 'obvious' is so elusive – and what to do about something we all know, but still get wrong.

Because obvious it may be, but mistakes are ubiquitous, the stakes are often high and spotting what's missing in the real world is maddeningly elusive. It evades thousands who are expressly looking for it, and the examples in the smart-thinking lit – in business, politics, data, everywhere – can be jaw-dropping. 'How the hell did they miss that,' you ask, 'when it's so obvious this was exactly the kind of problem they should have been looking for?'

What's missing is hardest to spot when everyone's focused on the gate, and only the gate; when the media have the gate in the crosshairs, and questions are asked in Parliament about the gate, after the sheep escaped. Was the gate open or closed? Who oiled the hinges and maintained the gate? Who paid for the gate? Was this gate unfettered capitalism? Is it woke?

So one way into the problem is to say that it's only partly about what we miss; it's also about how we focus, because although focus is often good, it can also be a distraction. We'll see how focus can be biased, ruinous and lethal. The books are full of stories about how it's the perspectives we take that cause us to overlook those that matter more.

Another way of tackling the problem is by saying that in a way it hardly makes sense: how do we spot what we can't see? Our ignorance tends to be invisible to us.[2] Blind spots, by definition, are things we're blind to. It's like the fish-in-water problem – how does it know it's in water when it doesn't know there's anything else? A second picture of the same scene shows the problem as we live it, the view before the big reveal of hindsight. Now where should you focus?

Evidence is always partial. Facts are not truth, though they are part of it – information is not knowledge.

Hilary Mantel

'Hey, like my gate? Nice gate, huh?' Etc. 'What's that? Springs maybe a touch rusty? Well spotted, thanks for your focus, I'll see they're oiled.'

You see the problem. So how do we see what we can't? Here are some ideas...

Writing about the global financial crash, Gillian Tett, one of the few to see it coming, said, 'Listen for the social silence, not just the noise.' Listen for what people don't talk about:

All the chatter in financial media was about equity markets (stocks and shares), but the activity driving revenue was derivatives (contracts based on an asset like a house or a share, but not the thing itself, more like a bet on what the thing will be worth in the future, for example). There was almost zero coverage on these... and so in a way the noise was the equity markets, and the silence was the derivatives market. I decided to refocus coverage onto derivatives.

Derivatives contracts worldwide were worth trillions, often run by a few people in a small corner of a bank, or in below-the-radar institutions now known as shadow banking. When derivatives prices crashed, this destroyed some of the richest companies in the world, brought famous banks close to ruin, led to a deep recession, vast government bailouts and borrowing and, in the UK, 'austerity'.

Inside those banks were risk managers whose job was to look for exactly this kind of risk, and executives who were supposed to know their business. How did they miss it? They lacked imagination for the bigger picture, some

> said; they were too accustomed to looking at things in one
> standard way, said others. They didn't think about their
> own mental models of how the world worked.

What do we tend to be silent about? Gillian says it's the things we take for granted, or the assumptions everyone shares. Or we ignore the 'embarrassing, self-evident, taboo, geeky or dull'. Or because we work and think in silos, we fail to see connections – the department of gates doesn't talk to the department of fences. 'Tunnel vision is deadly. We need lateral vision,' says Gillian. 'If you take a photograph, your eyes will be trained to go to the centre of the image. But what is around that? What are you screening out, and therefore what are you not seeing?' A tip, she says, is to look at the world as an alien would, trying to make everything that's familiar strange.[3]

Another take on missing what matters: David Hand's *Dark Data*. Dark data are information or evidence that people overlook or can't easily see, not realizing what they're missing. David's book is packed with costly destructive cases. Here's one you could almost call a favourite of his, except it's so horrifying.

> When the Challenger *Space Shuttle exploded, killing the
> seven crew, the proximate cause was failure of a rubber-
> like seal called an O-ring. There'd been suspicion that
> O-rings could fail in the cold and it was a bitter 2°C that
> day. But the team checked previous Shuttle flights when
> O-rings had shown hints of distress and found no clear
> pattern around temperature. So... they launched.*
>
> > *But they'd analysed only launches when they'd subse-
> quently found signs of a problem. They didn't check
> launches that were O-ring problem-free. Why bother*

> *checking if nothing happened? Because had they looked,
> they'd have found that whenever the O-rings were fine –
> whenever nothing happened – it was far likelier to be warm.
> Whenever something did happen, it was far, far likelier to
> be cold. Suddenly the relationship was clear. Warmer was
> safer, after all. And if warm was safer, then cold...*
>
> *The moment of realization must have been heart-
> stopping. But who thinks to look at what happens, when
> nothing happens? Except that nothing in this case is
> exactly what you want to happen, so you should abso-
> lutely be interested in the conditions that help nothing
> to happen. When you plot all the data on a graph and
> put the warm, problem-free events with O-ring distress
> events, the pattern is clear and 2°C goes off the chart for
> danger. A later inquiry concluded that the temperature
> that day made O-ring distress 'almost a certainty'.*

David Hand describes fifteen types of dark data, classify-
ing this one mainly as DD type 2: 'Data We Don't Know Are
Missing'. What use is big data if it's missing the critical part?
You can analyse the data all you like – it won't help.

Other reasons for ignoring data include: 'We didn't have
any, so what else are we supposed to do', 'We already have
enough data', 'We already have *all* the data' (meaning all that's
available) and 'Why would I look at that?'

> *In* Invisible Women, *Caroline Criado Perez exposed the
> 'data bias in a world designed for men', in medicine,
> research and elsewhere: for example, that women are
> 50 per cent more likely to be misdiagnosed after a heart
> attack. Crash dummies were, until recently, based on an*

*What we are familiar with
we cease to see.*

Anaïs Nin (via Gillian Tett)

Volvo's digital, dark-skinned, pregnant crash dummy really doesn't
want to miss anything. Is it an overdose of awareness, or a good
reminder not to presume?

> average male or a child, not on an average female. How
> did we not see what we were missing?
>
> When Chidiebere Ibe, a medical student and illus-
> trator, depicted a black foetus in the womb that went
> viral in 2021, the reaction was overwhelming, he said.
> Partly, it was shock – people saying: 'I never realized that
> we never see this.' Medical illustrations are, by default,
> white and – when possible – male, Chidiebere says. How
> didn't more of us notice until 2021? Just when you begin
> to think you see such things better, you wonder if you've
> started.[4]

They're unnerving, these pictures that disrupt our usual focus; they suggest familiarity can be a con, 'normal' an anaesthetic. Maybe it's simply habit that plays a part (as well as bias or prejudice) in causing the data neglect of women, the economy to crash, the *Challenger* to blow up.

To Matthew Syed in *Rebel Ideas*, that suggests a strat-egy. Think again about seeing our blind spots. Not easy – by definition. We can't expect to see what we don't see. Asking *yourself* what you're missing can even miss the point, although there's an entertaining sub-thread from Margaret Heffernan that we also miss what we can see all too well but choose not to, maybe because it's not welcome. *Wilful Blindness*, she calls it. Whatever the root of our selective attention, if we're serious about lessening the risks, then we need to start with what Margaret calls a 'fierce deter-mination to see'. And to put that determination to see into practice, smart-thinking's biggest idea is simple: fresh eyes (aka 'viewpoint diversity').

But properly fresh, not just more of the same. If you want rebel ideas, find rebels, is the crux of it. Seek out people who look differently, people with different backgrounds or disciplines, someone who knows how data can fail, not simply the boosters with flashy analytics to sell. Maybe hire an anthropologist like Gillian Tett, trained to look for what's not seen but is often assumed (some companies have done exactly that). Matthew says organizations are often run by clones, near enough – same background, same perspective, clever maybe, but thoughts on all the same rails. He urges for more diversity as an optimizing strategy, not just a social responsibility. He asks why organizations make a totem of 'the way we do things around here', why decisions are taken in meetings where one or two people dominate, why so many of us prefer the views of the like-minded. It all inhibits viewpoint diversity.

Do you treat dissent as a threat to your status? Why do we create hierarchies that minimize challenge? Why not – to take an idea from elsewhere – employ red teams whose job is expressly to look for what's missed or wrong and who have the power and freedom to go after it? Oh, we find reasons. We talk of cohesion, focus, common purpose, a shared narrative. But Matthew, Gillian, Margaret and co. have a point. Unless we're specifically organized to refocus, will we?

James Surowiecki, in *The Wisdom of Crowds*: *Why the Many are Smarter Than the Few*, says diverse, independent thinking is the core of that whole idea. If a crowd is gathered, homogenous and coordinated, or dominated, it might have no more wisdom than one numpty alone. Diversity and independence are what make the crowd wise. His book has become a classic.

One way of encouraging this diversity, James says, is decentralization: 'Decentralization's great strength is that it encourages independence and specialization on the one hand while still allowing people to coordinate their activities and solve difficult problems on the other.' But – there's always a 'but' – 'Decentralization's great weakness is that there's no guarantee that valuable information that's uncovered in one part of the system will find its way into the rest of the system.'

A personal opinion. I'm a non-exec director of a hospital. In healthcare, we measure to the nth everything about patient safety and quality of care. And so we should. Not least, we're told to or else. We monitor survival, errors, falls, complaints, how well we do basic checks; we monitor staffing ratios, survey satisfaction, and on it goes; and this helps keep patients safe.

What's missing? A heap of patient safety not routinely even called safety. What we hardly measure in healthcare is what happens to patients still waiting for treatment. How often do they die, or deteriorate and become harder to treat, how often is recovery longer, or the op longer or less effective because they sat so long on a list? How much grief or hardship, stress, mental ill health did it cause, including for work or family? Only the vaguest idea, and I work there. This is all patient risk and safety, all of it harm, but by comparison we hardly see it.

Instead we talk about dealing with waiting as 'responsiveness', which sounds like how you'd rate a call centre – how long it takes to serve the customer. When Covid-19 hit, that began to change, as it became clear that hospitals chock-full of Covid patients meant a huge and growing backlog. But still we had only a limited handle on the consequences. The reason? Mainly visibility. If you're inside a hospital, you're easy to see. If you're a patient outside, your safety is not a salient metric. Data-wise, it's one of Gillian's social silences. Safety that you can see and count easily gets counted, and what's counted tends to count, an old adage goes.

I don't know how this difference between patients before and after they walk through the door is defensible. Not that fixing it or gathering the data would be easy. And I don't mean nobody cares. We care passionately. But somehow we have a system full of caring people who desperately want to help patients, but it's a system largely in the dark about how half of it performs. Does this cause us to prioritize safety inside, ahead of speed of treatment, with a net health cost to patients? Again, no idea.[5]

We miss things. We miss the degree to which we miss things. Do we also miss how much missing things is inevitable? We all need a better game plan, which starts by acknowledging how wicked the problem is and then: a) organizes against it; and b) expects to adapt when things don't turn out as expected (because of what we missed).

One last miss. On 5 August 2010 thirty-three Chilean miners were trapped by a cave-in. The rescue effort was herculean and cost an estimated $10–20 million. But why, when the government and the international donors and agencies who supported the rescue had failed in the past to pay for much cheaper safety improvements, was the money and effort suddenly to hand? Part of the answer is that the victims now had names, faces and families. Before, when the risk was known but not realized, no one knew who the victims would be. At this point they were what we might call 'statistical lives', not identified lives, and nothing was done. 'Statistical' lives often disappear from view. We miss them because we can't name them.

It's a problem in health screening. Those screened and treated for a dangerous disease who survive feel saved, and often say so. Some really are. They're highly visible. We might know their names. But some of these grateful survivors didn't need saving – screening is imperfect and produces false positives – meaning that they'd have survived anyway without treatment. We know these false positives are there statistically, but often we don't know who they are. They can't speak up because they don't know, either. In fact because they think they were saved, they speak up for screening that they would have been better without. As a result, we underestimate screening's potential harms from unnecessary treatment. Publicity material for screening used to ignore this problem. Although that's improved, it's still hard to raise aware-ness of the fate of people we can't see – the anonymous 'statistical' lives that are as real as anyone's.

Try this

A classic – almost a cliché – and you might know it. This picture has become an in-joke about a particular kind of thinking. Here's what it means...

In the Second World War the US military had to decide where to put armour on planes. Armour is heavy, so you can't answer 'everywhere'. You must use it wisely. This image famously represents where most enemy hits were supposedly found (though it was drawn in 2016).

And that looks like the full extent of the data – or all that you have. So, what's the answer? Where should you put more armour and why? Clue, think about what's missing.

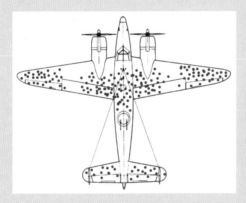

You can't answer the question without going outside the question.

David Spiegelhalter

Answer: put the armour where there are no holes. If people shooting at planes in mayhem hit them randomly – as you'd expect – why aren't there holes everywhere? Some holes are missing. Where are these missing holes? On the missing planes, the ones that didn't make it back. Why didn't they come back? Because they were hit where a hit was most dangerous, and that's where you most want the armour: where the observed holes aren't.

This is a real story. Abraham Wald worked for the Statistical Research Group, a US military-intelligence agency in the Second World War. This was his answer, and they acted on it. You can read more in Jordan Ellenberg's *How Not to Be Wrong*, about 'the hidden maths of every-day life', though not sure I'd call this maths.

The problem is sometimes called 'survivor bias': we only see the survivors. 'Secrets of success' books – even some of the most acclaimed – are plagued by survivor bias, looking only at what the successful company did. They often miss the business failures that might have relied on the same supposed secrets.

Not so fast

Now that you're sensitive to the risk of missing things, go back to Chapter 5 to rethink the danger of seeing things that aren't there. As usual, one risk has a countervailing risk. If you're too sure there are missing things to be found, you might find them whether they're there or not.

Next, bear in mind while you're dissing silos, insisting that we need to break them down and look laterally, that some people think you're just spouting fashionable tosh. If by 'silos' you mean small teams with clear and concise objectives, they say, what's not to like? More, please! Where you see myopia and dysfunction, they see structure, focus and efficiency. Anyway where do you keep grain, if not in a silo?

So, silos or anti-silos? Which, when? Yet again, your smart is another's dumb, and we finish up with: it depends. That's not a dead end, but it is a trickier argument.

Next, to avoid missing anything critical, what'll you do: think of everything? Yes, says Cassie Kozyrkov, Google's chief decision scientist, who I think about as smart as they come and who once said: 'Before we ask whether you should do A or B, I want to know that you thought of the whole universe pretty much.'

In some contexts, she's probably right. Except that the annoying voice pipes up to say: in others, probably not. No one thinks of everything, not even a team, and think how much thinking time would be wasted. Then again, unless you consider everything, how do you know what you're missing?

Which is to say: how much should you invest in looking around, rethinking and refocusing, and when should you go with what you know? In *Algorithms to Live By*, Brian Christian and Tom Griffiths make a related distinction between 'explore' and 'exploit'. How long do you reconsider and when do you commit? Rethink, refocus and explore or get on with it? More of one can mean less of the other. In other words, seeking what's missing is not a free lunch. We're trading opportunity cost (what we could be doing if we weren't so focused on X) and what I have seen called 'optionality cost' (what we could achieve if we weren't sitting on the fence, trying to keep open options B–Z or wondering if there were others we hadn't even thought of). If you spend all your time looking for what's missing, you might fail to make progress when nothing was missing at all.

Take Covid-19, which at times felt like one long explore–exploit dilemma: use the vaccine we have now or stop to check out those blood clots? Explore or exploit? On lockdown, go hard early or wait for more data about what the virus is up to and what the lockdown options would mean, who they affect and how badly? With the first lockdown in the UK, the majority view seems to be that we waited too long; with Omicron, a later variant, that not acting hastily was right and we rode it out – though arguments still rage on all sides. There's no easy answer, no sure way to know how hard you should look or how long – though some argue that you should at least impose a stopping rule.

You can't keep your options open for ever. The longer you try and the more you bet on finding a better option, the more you might lose by not committing. Strangely, the 'miss lit' tends not to tell stories about people who spent an age faffing around and it was all wasted.

Because let's not forget that at some point focus can be a virtue: stay on task, we say, keep your eye on the ball. Commitment to a common purpose often matters, while encouraging viewpoint diversity might make us chaotic and distracted. Anyway, what do we think we'll get from a bunch of outsiders asking damn-fool questions? Often naivety, dead ends, wasted time and effort. Can we say with confidence that being single-minded never paid off?

So which is it: focus, or refocus? Both (this book is so annoying). This is a trade-off (another one), a balance of time and attention between focus and refocus, with no right or smart-thinking answer, just a bunch of hazard lights and, if we're lucky, opportunities in all directions. When do you go all-in? Or don't you? When do you look around? Once every five years when you do the corporate strategy?

At the very least we can remember there's a choice. Next, it's likely to be a better choice, and the looking for what's missing will be more efficient if we're aware of the technical blind spots in our reactions to evidence – like David Hand's revealing examples of dark data. So it really is worth reading more, learning about the kinds of things we miss and how,[6] so long as we balance this with a sense of the costs of looking.

One last 'but'. With so many people missing so much, the accusation is easy: 'You're missing something!' Such as: 'Those wind-farm people are missing that the wind sometimes stops.' Are they? You really think they never thought of that? Maybe you're the one missing something. A tip from Darren Dahly, a statistician: 'If you've spotted a major flaw in thinking that affects an area other smart people have been working on for decades, I recommend that you... keep reading until you've figured out what you're missing.' As before, use this book on your own thinking first – not to throw at others or you're missing the point.

Jargon

- **WYSIATI** or **What You See Is All There Is**: when we focus on the information we have as if it's all there is to know. An acronym from Daniel Kahneman.

- **Streetlight effect**: seeking opportunities only where they're obvious, under the light, and missing stuff in the darkness.

8

Draw the tiger

Own your ignorance

Know what a tiger looks like? Sure you do. Everyone does. You've seen *Tiger King*, you've been to the zoo. Fill in the stripes.

We'll let you off the face – it's tricky. But the stripes on the legs... come on, up and down or around? (Answer, page 145.) Pick up a pencil, deface the book if it's yours (or buy another!) and demonstrate that you know what everyone knows.

If you're normal, you'll pause and cogs will be grinding. Suddenly you're not so sure you do know what a tiger looks after all.[1] Hey, how stupid are you?

'But I do, I do, sort of. Just not... so much. Give me a moment, will ya?'

Don't worry, common misconception. What we really mean is that we know one if we see one. We think that means we know, but do we? *The Knowledge Illusion*, by Steven Sloman and Philip Fernbach, dives in. They describe a quick test of what's known as the 'illusion of explanatory depth' (devised by Frank Keil and Leon Rozenblit). That's when we think we know, but don't know much. It goes like this.

1. How well do you understand how a zip works? Rate your understanding 1–7.
2. *Explain* how a zip works.
3. Rate your understanding again.

Typically, scores at the first stage go down in the third. Add more questions seeking more detailed knowledge and the scores drop further. When forced to prove that we understand, we discover we don't. They say this shows how we live an illusion, by our own admission. 'When people rated their knowledge lower the second time, they were essentially saying, "I know less than I thought."' It's the same if you ask about something more elaborate than zips, like political policies.

The good news is that when confronted by evidence of our ignorance, we do at least recalibrate our estimation of what we know. We may be dumb, but we can be smart about recognizing it. Whether that changes our attitude to the next thing we think we know is something else.

Another benefit: people who feel unsure about what they know apparently pay more attention to people they think genuinely do know. When we learn more about our ignorance, we listen more; we become more curious (see Chapter 14). Part of this book's paradoxical purpose is that you could become smarter by putting it down at the end and saying, 'Me? I know nothing.' Now that would be an achievement. Well, not quite, but you see what I mean.

The next picture shows an outline of a bike – sort of, minus bits. The pictures below it are how a bunch of undergrads filled in a few more basics for Rebecca Lawson, a psychologist. If you ride much, you'll wet yourself. They're hilarious (so bad they can't be true, I thought – until I tried this on some of my family: 'Er, doesn't it have a... you know, somewhere around... somewhere?').

Just because you have imposter syndrome doesn't mean you aren't incompetent.

Daniel Lakens

Stop laughing, especially you cyclistas at the back. This is you – the minute you wander off the track of your own expertise. Or at least be sure to snigger equally at your own ignorance about all the other things you vaguely think you know.

Frankly, I'd say a lot of the knowledge-calibration in public argument is screwy like this. Too many loud voices only *think* they know. I think they should be less sure. We're all comically ignorant. Own it. Take the one virtue that comes from this exercise: learn to recalibrate.

All of which suggests a handy sense-check: if you think you know, draw the picture – a sometimes useful way of finding out what you don't (akin to advice that the best way to learn a subject is to write about it).

Later we'll look more at how far our casual knowledge runs, at how often we genuinely know what we're talking about when we say that one thing leads to another. The answer, typically, is not far. We sometimes know how stuff works that we're close to or work with directly. Beyond that, er...

The next question is how we kid ourselves otherwise. One answer seems to be that we think we know how a zip works, because we use zips. We mistake familiarity for understanding. Another answer begins with thinking things are simple – 'How hard can it be?' – because we're too ignorant about the subject to know it's complicated. If we faced up honestly to the complexity, maybe we'd find it unnerving,[2] so we look away. Now there's an easy strategy for you: avoid feeling ignorant by assuming you know it all. Let me know how that works out for ya.

'We ignore complexity by overestimating how much we know about how things work... We tell ourselves that we understand what's going on, that our opinions are justified by our knowledge, and that our actions are grounded in justified beliefs even though they are not. We tolerate complexity by failing to recognize it. That's the illusion of understanding,' say Steven Sloman and Philip Fernbach.

Though you have to ask: how do they know? And how do we know they're not kidding themselves, suffering from that same illusion of knowledge? Well, they study this, for one. They ride this bike, professionally, and I think they know what they're talking about. Expertise often counts for something, though there'll be more to say about that later.

Stripes on tigers and bits of bikes are at the shallow end of expertise, and a lot of us are already out of our depth. That should be a warning about the deep end. 'We all have domains in which we are experts, in which we know a lot in exquisite detail. But on most subjects... what we know is little more than a feeling of understanding we can't really unpack.'

On this account, it would be wise to admit our limitations before sounding off. Reminds me of a poem by Wendy Cope with a line about an easy cure for love: 'get to know him better,' she writes. The easy cure for confidence that you know a subject is to get to know it better.

All that said, I think I sense a little kickback, which goes like this: who cares about the stripes on a tiger or the structure of a bike? Sod that, it's trivial. All this knowledge-illusion business is irrelevant, because why would I even want to know this stuff? Here's what really matters: that I know about the things that really matter.

Fair enough. But do you? If bikes and tigers don't feel like relevant knowledge to you, so you don't care, take a different kind of knowledge, a similar problem, and dip into the smart-thinking sub-genre about how pig-ignorant we are of basic facts about the world around us – the kind of things people argue about because they say they care a lot. In *The Perils of Perception*, Bobby Duffy, who used to be at pollster Ipsos Mori, catalogued our ignorance.

The British, for example, think 15 per cent of their population is Muslim (actually 4.8 per cent). We think 43 per cent of young adults live at home (14 per cent). We overestimate, crazily, murder rates and teen pregnancies. We believe, impossibly, that men have three times as many sexual relationships on average as women. And on it goes. Bobby's subtitle? 'Why we're wrong about nearly everything.'

He produced a similar eye-opener with *The Generation Divide: Why We Can't Agree and Why We Should*, which ripped into the idea that boomers and millennials have radically different cultural attitudes or behaviours simply because of their date of birth. It's easy to find these assertions: that we're like this and they're like that. It's mostly ignorance talking (except about generations and money – odd stuff going on there), a great slew of assumptions that are generally unreliable, according to Bobby, and he seems to know his stuff. The rest of us, apparently, have been making it up, telling stories, thinking we know.

Then in *Factfulness*, Hans Rosling asked a few multiple-choice questions about global facts and trends. Such as…

1. What proportion of girls in developing countries finish primary school: 20 per cent, 40 per cent, 60 per cent ?

2. In the last twenty years, the proportion of the world population living in extreme poverty has: almost doubled, remained about same, almost halved?

3. There are two billion children aged 0–15. How many will there be in 2100, according to the UN: four billion, three billion, two billion?

4. How did the number of deaths from natural disasters change over the last 100 years: more than doubled, remained about the same, fell to less than half?

Answers: 1 60 per cent; 2 halved; 3 two billion; 4 halved.

Hans tried this on some smart audiences over the years, tech-savvy, intellectual, politically engaged. Their estimates of global facts and trends were worse than a chimp answering at random. That takes some doing. It means we're not just ignorant, we're ignorant while arrogantly thinking ourselves smart – otherwise we'd simply guess, like the chimps, and improve our score. Shown their results, those audiences laughed. In shame... despair? Not sure. It is kind of funny, but also kind of desperate. Like I say, they were clever and knowledgeable – inside their own zone. But stray outside and they're lost. Most of us are.

That leads Steven Sloman and Philip Fernbach to a suggestion for dealing with the burden of knowledge: share it out. No one can know it all, and those who think they do are soon embarrassed. Lean on others' expertise, use your own where you have it and listen more when you don't. Expertise is a community, they say, in which lots of us have little domains. Consequently, diverse teams work best (that one again). Their subtitle is: 'The myth of individual thought and the power of collective wisdom'.

Their book is partly a crash course in the need for what philosophers call epistemic humility (knowledge humble-pie to you and me). And, boy, on this evidence do we seem to need it. But the other point is that knowing only a few things properly can be an efficient way to organize (so now pause for a second to think of a reason why it could also be a bad idea).

One last thing amid all this ignorance. Another way to deal with it is to make assumptions. As Cassie Kozyrkov says: 'Assumptions are ugly band-aids you put over the parts where information is missing.' They can also be part of the knowledge illusion: we don't know, so we assume, and we assume our assumptions are good enough, or maybe forget we're making them. Like guesses and bets, assumptions are unavoidable, but it sure helps to know how much hangs on them, and how fragile they are. Cassie says write down explicitly all the assumptions you make as you work towards a conclusion, try to catch yourself at it.

Not so fast

Two big objections to the claim we're all ignorant:

First, humans have a superb 'need-to-know' filter (we've touched on this). Who cares which way the frickin' stripes go? I know a tiger when I see one. Poverty, I do care about, but how much detail do I need? Poverty's bad, I want our leaders on it – enough.

But is that enough? There are a lot of ways of tackling poverty. Do some work better than others? Do some make the problem worse? What if our leaders are on it the wrong way? How far can we surrender judgement to others?

The hitch comes when more detailed knowledge matters, but still we know next to nothing. 'Know your limits' is the metacognition advice in that event, so that we know when we need help. But how can we know how limited we are without knowing the subject's complexities?

In the end, we finish up with nothing stronger than this assumption: there's very often more to it than we can see from the outside. Since we can't know whether that hidden detail is going to matter, it's probably, usually best to take our confidence down a notch or two, maybe expect a few things to come back and bite us, and assume there's more to it than we initially see. Maybe, possibly, consult a few domain experts?

Except... next comes the second big objection to the claim we're ignorant. OK, maybe we are — more ignorant even than chimps guessing at random. But experts can also be as ignorant as chimps guessing at random. In *Expert Political Judgement: How Good Is It?* Philip Tetlock reported a thirty-year study of expert prediction that found they were 'about as accurate as a chimp throwing darts'.[3]

This is not looking good. Stray from your own expertise and you're beaten by a chimp; stick with the experts and they're comparable to a chimp. OK, so we're beset with knowledge illusions, but it can't all be chimps, can it?

Worse, all those experts in the science replication crisis haven't exactly brought glory to expertise. And... Philip's next book, *Superforecasting*, written with Dan Gardner, showed that a few reflective, disciplined amateur generalists could beat expert forecasters.

How do we reconcile *The Knowledge Illusion* and its endorsement of expertise with Philip's reasons for scepticism about experts and the superior performance of his team of amateurs? Partly, we read Chapter 13, that's how, which is about the problem of expertise and who you can trust. Bear in mind, meanwhile, that Philip repeatedly warns that his findings about expert *forecasting* should not be used to dismiss expertise in general. Note, too, who we're relying on to judge when you can trust expertise: Philip Tetlock, an expert in expert judgement. It's not you (or me). And when experts do struggle, that alone doesn't make you somehow *more* expert than they are. When in doubt, I'd say err towards humility. But what do I know?

Try this

Quick self-test. Pick someone you disagree with. How well do you know their views? Do you really get why they think like that? Is your only explanation for their opinions that they are evil, self-interested or lying? Or is it just possible that there's something about their position that you don't fully appreciate? If your understanding of 'them' is as good as your understanding of a zip, maybe learn more about them.

Jargon

- *Dunning–Kruger effect*: the tendency for people who know least to be worst at estimating their knowledge – usually to think they know more than they do (after research by David Dunning and Justin Kruger). Take care, there's a gorgeous tendency to cite this as 'the most confident know the least', which isn't what it says at all. Say that and you're an example of Dunning–Kruger. Next klaxon warning: the Dunning–Kruger effect might not exist. The research on which it's based was challenged by a paper in 2016 that suggested the finding was statistically flawed.[4] I think the critics have a point. So, is Dunning–Kruger a brilliant example of Dunning–Kruger? I'll leave that one here. If that doesn't make you careful, nothing will. 'The first rule of the Dunning–Kruger club,' said Dave Dunning, 'is that you don't know you're a member of the Dunning–Kruger club.'

Stripes

On the back legs, tiger stripes go around, becoming more diagonal at the top as they change from horizontal on the legs to the vertical stripes on the body. I'll give you one point if you said 'horizontal' or 'around'.

Another point if you said the front legs are different, even if you didn't know how. There the stripes go horizontally across the back, but most tigers don't really have stripes on the front of the front legs – maybe a wispy diagonal line here or there.

A third point if you were right about both front and back of the front legs. How did you do? I scored one out of three.

How to draw an owl

1.

2.

1. Draw some circles   2. Draw the rest of the f***ing owl

It's like this. Original source for this lost in time; whoever did it, *chapeau*.[1]

9

Mind your pictures

The sketchpad in the head

As we were saying, the world is infinite, and you and I have about a thimbleful of knowledge each. Point taken, suitably humbled.[2]

But don't despair, my friend, all's not lost just because you're pig-ignorant about almost everything. We can spread the burden of knowing by specializing. We'll each do our bit and draw from other people's thimbles when we're lacking. Teamwork again, and why this book takes from many others – because knowledge is collective. Between us, we make the most of the brains we have.

But there's another strategy for eking out mental capacity that's more than efficient; it's the ultimate in smart. Predictably, if it goes wrong, it's the ultimate in stupid, too. Worse, there's no opting out, we must all do it – aiming high, risking the intellectual gutter.

And here it is: simplify... and generalize.

Sod the precise stripes of the tiger, forget the detail; nail the essentials, as this book also tries to do. In essence, look for the essence – cut through complexity to find the broad outlines or salient features. Look, tigers are striped; enough.

The smart in finding the essence of things is that what's essentially true in one case is often true in others – only the details differ. No need for a different name or conception for every variety of chair so long as we recognize its essential chair-ness, which means we know where to sit. Knowledge of this kind generalizes, like a skeleton key to many locks. It suggests that life has an underlying structure of repeated patterns and significant features – which it's the dream of science to discover. It's also what teachers wish the class would grasp sooner than the umpteenth example. Knowing that things are of a type (across place, history, in business, life) is deep knowledge. One way to talk about these essences is to call them models.

'Instead of relying on fickle and specialized facts, we can learn versatile concepts,' says the Farnham Street blog about mental models.[3] 'History doesn't repeat itself but it does rhyme,' say Gabriel Weinberg and Lauren McCann in *Super Thinking: The Big Book of Mental Models*. 'If you can identify a mental model that applies to the situation in front of you, then you immediately know a lot about it,' write Shane Parrish and Rhiannon Beaubien.[4]

So far, so clever. The problem starts with that little 'if'. '*If* you can identify a mental model...'

Which model, which essence? How do you know you've extracted the right one from a wickedly complicated world? Models, theories, generalizations, principles, the normal, simplifying assumptions of science, are all trying to extract the right essence.[5]

Before long, in fact, you begin to wonder if this simplifying, essence-extraction game is what all thinking is.[6] You can't fit the whole world in your head – you have to be choosy. And we can say that without going anywhere near the deep philosophy about whether thoughts correspond to real things out there. Let's take for granted that they do; there are still too many real things to take in, we've no choice but to be selective and simplify.

Forced then to ignore the snowstorm of detail, we must be like those experts who create more formal mathematical models of disease or the economy: not a model containing you and me and the candlestick-maker and all our dreams, but a simplified model – a 'sketchpad in the head' – of how key features fit together, those we think matter.

We'll use this word 'model' as shorthand for all the ways we do this, formal or unconscious.[7] Huge simplification, but there you go; what else do we do?

In the owl-circles picture, the two rough circles stand for all those models. This is your mental sketchpad. They're not the thing itself, obviously, but they catch enough essence to be useful, we hope.[8] Every political policy, every hypothesis, every plan, every idea is a drawing of circles. Their weakness? The picture makes it clear: the risk of being *too* simple, or simple in the wrong way.

Life, meanwhile, with its mass of complication, is here in all the gorgeous detail of the 'f-----g owl'. Thinking would be better if we could mentally sketch all this detail faithfully, but that's a tall order when we don't have head-space for the stripes of a tiger, and every owl is different. But out there beyond our mental sketchpads, that's how life is: intricately feathered.

And that's the struggle, folks: simplify because we must, extract the essentials because they can reveal deeper truths, just don't miss anything that's going to matter. Run along now.[9]

James George Frazer, an anthropologist at the end of the nineteenth century, put it like this in *The Golden Bough*:

The propensity to excessive simplification is indeed natural to the mind of man, since it is only by abstraction and generalisation, which necessarily imply the neglect of a multitude of particulars, that we can stretch our puny faculties so as to embrace a minute portion of the illimitable vastness of the universe... If this propensity is natural and even inevitable, it is nevertheless fraught with peril, since it is apt to narrow and falsify our conception of any subject under investigation.

And here's John Kay, one of my favourite thinkers:

Physicists describe motion on frictionless planes, gravity in a world without air resistance. Not because anyone believes that the world is frictionless and airless, but because it is too difficult to study everything at once. A simplifying model eliminates confounding factors and focuses on a particular issue of interest.[10]

The principle is sound, unavoidable even. But it's fraught with the 'peril', as James George Frazer put it, of choosing the wrong simplicity, or not including a detail that proves critical.

> Covid modelling was urgent, necessary and spot-on at times; at others, from a practical viewpoint, it was vaguer than two circles sketched drunk in the dark.
>
> On 26 July 2021 the Centers for Disease Control in the US issued forecasts for cases of Covid-19 by twenty-seven modelling groups, including Microsoft, Facebook AI Research, the Los Alamos National Laboratory, various universities, etc.
>
> Their expert judgement was all over the shop. For the week ending 14 August, four weeks ahead, forecasts ranged from a little over 10,000 cases a day to about 100,000. One outlier said a million. Was the epidemic dying out or about to explode? Couldn't say. How the models stood in relation to the f-----g owl was almost anyone's guess at that point. Critics said this was bad modelling. But was that fair? Was

the problem the model or was it the nature of this owl? Were we expecting the model to know what couldn't be known? A more serious objection was that each model wasn't sufficiently uncertain – all of them claiming more accuracy than was plausible.

It's hellish hard to model a disease by taking a few key numbers that often change and are estimates anyway. Plus, how things turn out can depend on what the government might do, which the model doesn't pretend to know yet; or on people's behaviour, which changes with events and then affects the spread of the epidemic. Then there's the problem that the bug kept reinventing itself.

Essences give an impression of being timeless. But we didn't know by the next month which beast we were meant to model. So spare a thought for modellers... as long as they show humility and uncertainty and state their assumptions. When they do, pay attention, because maybe they've found an essential.

Think of the problem like a rocky marriage between Essence and Detail. Essence wants a simple life – it brings clarity – but can be aloof and patronizing. Detail is particular and precise, and more than a little overbearing. 'Can't you see the big picture?' wails Essence; 'You don't know what it's like!' screams Detail.

Here are two angles on how we go wrong.

1. When the distance between essence and detail becomes too great:

   Economic modelling before the global financial crash was, with hindsight, scarcely on speaking terms with the

> economy itself, so far apart were assumptions about what could happen from what actually did. A massive transmission of investment risk rattling through the whole economy wasn't meant to be possible. But risk models were more than a few feathers short of the essentials – notably the central, contagious role of the banks and other financial institutions.
>
> More generally, according to John Kay, one of the dominant economic models at the time made the following assumptions, among others: 'everyone lives for two periods of equal length and works for one and spends in another; there is only one good, and no possibility of storage of that good, or of investment; there is only one homogenous kind of labour; there is no mechanism of family support between older and younger generations.' A useful sketch? Economists are still arguing.[11]

2. When we assume there isn't much distance between model and detail, perhaps forgetting that circles aren't owls; the essence of the thing and the thing itself, with all its granularity, can be a long way apart. Alfred Korzybski, a philosopher, put it like this: 'The map is not the territory'[12] – as pithy a statement of the problem as you'll find. Writers love that metaphor. The John Kay essay I quoted is called 'The Map is Not the Territory'. There's a series of short books about rational thinking called *A Map that Reflects the Territory*.

Demands a picture, don't you think? Here's a screen-grab of Google Maps' proof-of-the-pudding that maps and territory can be strangers, when it showed me routes to the theatre, including: jump from Waterloo Bridge on the River Thames, possibly onto a moving boat, possibly *into* the River Thames.

Everything we know about the world is a model. Every word and every language is a model. All maps and statistics, books and databases, equations and computer programmes are models. So are the ways I picture the world in my head – my mental models. None of these is or ever will be the real *world.*

Donella Meadows[13]

There's no scheduled stop for the boat at this point or even a pier/jetty, just a dotted line under the bridge. The map doesn't tell you these, erm... details, or how far down it is from bridge to river. Had Google been watching James Bond? And if I missed the boat? I think it says this route would take seven minutes more than walking more directly, but as this was midwinter and the Thames here is tidal, maybe longer – a lot longer.

But what's the alternative to maps? There's a (fictional) story or two about maps that lacked sufficient detail so they were expanded, and expanded again, until they reached a scale of 1:1, as big as the territory itself, when they were useless. You can't say it all. We need maps. We must simplify.

And not only 'must'. The right simplification can be genius. Sometimes the meanest model (modellers talk of 'parsimony' and 'compression') can predict sublimely the complexity of the real world. In *Life is Simple*, Johnjoe McFadden sees this simplicity as the golden thread running through scientific progress, the way to every great breakthrough from Copernicus to Darwin and Einstein, leading us towards the true, underlying simplicity of nature itself.[14]

In *Thinking Better*, Marcus du Sautoy says one of the best tools for spotting and abstracting essences is maths, which gives us mean shortcuts to knowledge. Mathematical abstractions are brilliant for solving novel problems you've never seen before. And he has a point: all those simplifications of gravity that ignored the details of air resistance served us brilliantly everywhere we went (and still do, even after Einstein told us we'd misunderstood gravity). As Marcus also suggests, just about every kind of thinking about anything involves a variety of simplification or shortcut. The 'chair' example earlier is one of his. And that works, doesn't it, kinda?

Marcus even ventures on to maps. Brave man. One map – of the London Underground – is better for having less topographical detail, he says. People love its simplicity. Me, too; it's magnificently minimalist. Fine, says John Kay, just don't use it to travel from Paddington station to visit friends living near Lancaster Gate, as he did, to be met on arrival with laughter. Here's the Tube map. Paddington to Lancaster Gate, four stops, one change.

If it's simple, it's false. If it's complex, it's unusable.

Paul Valéry

And here's another map with selected extra topographical detail.

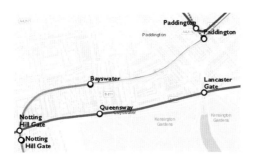

Far quicker to walk, and with less effort, as the locals know. The key with all models is not that they're wrong – they're all wrong in some way – but whether they help. The answer for the London Tube map is: usually.

There's a line in the philosophy of science that says what we need is not a map, but maps: 'a collection of maps, all of them incomplete, which together gradually shape our understanding of a new piece of country. By bringing those maps together and constantly improving them... in time we build up a composite picture which brings us closer and closer to what the outside world is telling us.'[15] Which sounds wise enough, until you think about how many maps you're willing to carry and consult.

In the smart-thinking struggle between essence and detail, some rave about the power of essence, the abstract ideas and principles that help us cut through; some fret over the loss of detail, the particulars that make all the difference. They all have stories: of success for their own vision, failure for the other. Tension between them is inevitable.

So who's right and what'll it be, essence or detail? As usual, both and neither. As the owl suggests, detail can be beyond us – there's too much world to take in. On the other hand, the very act of trying to make it more comprehensible by focusing on a few essentials makes it wrong. On the third hand, essence can be genius. On the fourth, detail can be everything, as we'll see in the next chapter.

Four hands? But when did we say this was easy? When you accept both the good and bad in models – mental or formal – opinions that seem contradictory begin to make sense. One modeller says formal models are stupid, but:

The stupidity of a model is often its strength. By focusing on some key aspects of a real-world system (i.e., those aspects instantiated in the model), we can investigate how such a system would work if, in principle, we really *could* ignore everything we are ignoring. This only sounds absurd until one recognizes that, in our theorizing about the nature of reality – both as scientists and as quotidian humans hopelessly entangled in myriad webs of connection and conflict – *we ignore things all the time.*[16]

Take that, all you smart-thinking worriers about what you might be missing. Good models also express their uncertainty. But since uncertainty strikes some as the antithesis of knowledge, this can cause misunderstanding, even anger. Yet it's vital to state the uncertainty in our models, because knowing our ignorance is a heck of a lot better than not knowing our ignorance.

For a sceptical approach, what matters most is a winter-sharp sense of the pros and cons of both model and detail, especially of moving from one perspective to another, from circles to owl and back. We can be horribly vague about how we make the jump between the two, and how they're linked is often a black box, sometimes even to the modellers, so it's worth trying to set out explicitly the steps we take – all the assumptions and judgements when we draw our sketch.

> *Weirdly, experts can be strangely vague about which bit of reality they're trying to represent – what are their circles meant to be? – at the same time as claiming they reveal general truths about, erm... something, an*

> *owl maybe. Sounds like they disappear up their own abstractions. It's a frequent complaint in research that people often aren't clear what question they're trying to answer – a problem sometimes known as 'problem uncertainty' or the difficulty of problem formulation. Getting the problem formulation right is harder than it sounds.*
>
> *A paper from Anna Scheel surveying psychology research, stated: 'The articles we analysed all claimed to provide evidence for (or against) something, but too often it was impossible to determine what exactly that something was, and which data would support or contradict it – the scientific claims were ill-defined.' These papers were 'not even wrong,' she said, adding: 'To produce scientific claims that are less elusive and more meaningful, we need to recognise the broken parts of our inference chains and then try to repair them.' That is, how exactly do your circles relate to life?*[17]

As usual here, there's complacency about our smarts: a little too much confidence that we've extracted the essence successfully. In extremis, this overconfidence can be catastrophic: we can have so much faith in the model that we think it's not a model, it's, you know, real, or even that it is what real should be; and then the danger is that we expect reality to make any necessary compromise, insist that it will – must – obey the sketchpad in our head, like ideologues or modernist central planners. Models that slide like this into becoming rules are a special threat: our ideas seem so logical that people in all their feathered complexity are bound to conform – of course they will – and should. 'The terrible simplifiers', Clive James called the visionaries who imposed totalitarian political models on the twentieth century, at a cost of millions of lives.[18] When the sketchpad in the head produces a bad sketch, it's not just passively bad; it can actively distort what we do.

Or, if you prefer, take another classic statement of the problem, the surrealist painter René Magritte's *The Treachery of Images*. The image isn't the real thing, folks, in case you're wondering what he was trying to say, maybe also laced with sexual innuendo (look it up).

We see life through models. We've no choice. It's all sketch-pads in the head.

This is old philosophy, but these pictures help remind us how fraught with hazards it is – and we need reminders. Reason about the model itself, not only what we think we see with it, because thinking is nothing if not self-aware (see Chapter 1). Circles and owl capture the distance between thought and thing, the 'roughly' of all thinking. So models, yes, of all kinds, necessary, sometimes revelatory. But don't mistake them for the 'f***ing owl' (or the pipe).

Footnote: it's sometimes said that AI can square the circle by taking account of massively more feathers than our puny human brains can. Then when the AI draws a sketch, it's more accurate, less abstract, and we can be more confident it has all the true essentials. All we need do is test its performance and, if it works, bingo – the model is good. Yeah, maybe, sometimes, for some purposes, with a lot of failures on the way and glitches that often materialize later. But bear in mind that models can be accurate without being correct, as Ptolemy's model of the solar system, with Earth at the centre, described what he saw pretty well – and was even reliably predictive... but wrong. Just because it works (up to a point) doesn't make it accurate. The problem is we might not know until too late if the AI has the right essentials or only looks like it, and really it's found a way to cheat. This happens. Weirdly, you can even have a model that's too accurate. It precisely matches the owls it was trained on, but there are varieties of owl it's not seen before, so it's not the generalizable model you think.[19]

Not so fast

First, you've already realized, I guess, that this chapter's picture/metaphor of a sketchpad in the head is itself a model. Who says it's a good one? Who says a sketchpad in the head is the best characterization of what goes on when we think about the outside world? As with all models, it's wrong. In fact, while we're on the point, *all* the pictures in this book suggest models of thinking and they're all in some way wrong. But are they useful? And even if they are, are they also misleading? That's the judgement we must make every time.

Second, it's tempting, but no defeatism or annoyance, if you please. Puny faculties we may have, the illimitable vastness of the universe is overwhelming, and models may be basically stupid and prone to failure while being at the same time the only way, and promising insight. But the best answer is not despair, or frustration, or great expectations, it's strategy. I like Philip Tetlock and Dan Gardner's formulation of what to do: mix what they call the inside and outside view,[20] switch between what's true in general (the basic circles and essentials of the model) and what's different this time in this place (the feathers and the particulars); 'between nitty gritty granular and big picture strategic abstractions'. Zoom in on detail, zoom out, repeat. Accept that there's seldom resolution.

It's not that both perspectives fail – though they do – it's that they epitomize those trade-offs we keep talking about, they have different uses, strengths and weaknesses. For example, models allow us to do thought experiments or surrogative reasoning, create what-if scenarios, and so on, without screwing up the real world.

Many of us prefer one perspective to the other: prefer theory, laws, models, the big picture and generalizations; or prefer detail, local context, nuts-and-bolts pragmatism, feathers. The best of Philip's superforecasters mix these up. It's those dragonfly eyes again (see page 28).[21]

Try this

Define the essentials in a chair. Not what you would like in a chair – the essentials. And not too many or you'll rule out obvious chairs. Then check the 'chairs' opposite. Did they meet your criteria, did you choose the right essentials?[22] Look up iconic chair designs and mull the competing claims of different schools to have defined their essence. 'With every design, the key is to discover what inhabits the object, uncover it, acknowledge it, so that anyone who encounters it will understand,' said Jacob Jensen, a designer. Go for it!

Essence of chair. 1 Bouloum lounge chair. 2 'Satirical seating' by Yanko Design (we'll have another use for this one later) – if it's not a chair, what is it? 3 Panton Chair by Vitra. 4 'Sitting rock', seen for sale online from a garden centre.

Jargon

- *Bonini's paradox*: 'As a model of a complex system becomes more complete, it becomes less understandable. Alternatively, as a model grows more realistic, it also becomes just as difficult to understand as the real-world processes it represents.' As described by John Dutton and William Starbuck.[23]

- *The fallacy of misplaced concreteness*: mistaking 'an abstract belief, opinion, or concept about the way things are for a physical or "concrete" reality' (from Wiki). See also 'the fallacy of reification'.

Course it'll work. A desire line in Vauxhall, London. Earliest known appearance in a tweet by Peter Fortune, a member of the London Assembly, who says whenever he works on a policy decision he thinks of this image.

10

Think bad thoughts

Expecting the unexpected

Fact: chicanes on footpaths make cyclists slow down, reducing accidents. Someone's modelled it, run trials of the real thing, has data – bet they do. On the strength of that, people make policies about chicanes and then off we pop to build them, because they work.

So, uh... yeah. And in this case, uh... no.

Improvised routes, like the bypassing of this chicane, are called desire lines: the popular will scrawled into the earth. The result can be worse than failure of the original plan – because the question in my mind is whether it's only cyclists who are scrawling their desires here. If so, at least we could say we'd safely separated bikes and pedestrians. But bike, buggy, wheelchair, pedestrian, scooter, mobility scooter, horse... Does anyone take the chicane any more? Skaters, maybe, or if it's wet or muddy. Or did we ruin the point of the whole footpath?

The planned, primary effect was to slow down certain people. The secondary effect was maybe that they didn't slow down because they didn't use the path, and now who does?

Desire lines are a neat metaphor for the human factor, one variety of the unplanned bolshiness of life. Before planning almost anything, beware the desire line.

Is it me or does this particular act of bolshiness look like a grin in the grass? It's life's two fingers to self-confidence, the kind of gremlin that leaves us saying the rules would work so much better if only people followed them, or 'I'd have got away with it, if it weren't for those pesky kids.'

We reason, analyse, gather evidence, have ideas, think them through, maybe test them, reflect on previous experience and, out of that, make policies and plans. We know they work because they work, and they're so logical anyway, what else would they do? Except when they don't. A sense for the many reasons they don't work belongs in the top tier of your thinking toolbox.

And why don't they? There are two broad, non-exclusive explanations: people and systems. The people explanation says someone was stupid, useless or just wrong, so blame them. It's simple, at least, and maybe satisfying, and that makes it tempting. It places the world's problems inside people's heads – a bit like some smart-thinking.

The system explanation is more frustrating, but at least as interesting, and that's what this chapter is about. It too has smart-thinking champions. As the statistician W. Edwards Deming said: 'A bad system will beat a good person every time.'[1] The system explanation says these screw-ups are 'the inevitable by-product of people doing the best they can in systems that themselves contain multiple subtle vulnerabilities'.[2]

Such as? One place to begin is with no-frills, everyday bad luck, to which we're all vulnerable. You had it all worked out, your business planning was prudent, all running nicely, then it was a windy day in Egypt and a container ship got stuck in the Suez Canal, and that was that: an estimated $400 million an hour of consequence. Not in anyone's forecasts, arguably not in their control, but hey-ho, colossal, and maybe ruinous for a few who you might say were blameless.[3] 'What do you expect *me* to do about the Suez Canal?'

One little thing. Tugs try to free the *Ever Given*,
a container ship stuck in the Suez Canal in 2021.

But there's more to this kickback than bad luck, and the varieties, which are legion, are worth a moment more of your thought. For example, there's the famed and much-lamented unintended consequence, which isn't quite bad luck, as it results directly from something you did, but you sure didn't mean to do *that*.

> *Daycare centres, hoping to improve parental punctuality at pick-up time, started fining parents who were late – except that the parents started treating the fine like a fee – and the lateness got worse. An ethical responsibility to show up on time had somehow been turned into a contractual entitlement to do the opposite. Oops. People, eh?*

Here's another:

> *I picked up a taste for unintended consequences as a young documentary maker when the anthropologist Mary Douglas told me a story about a tribe she'd studied that carried wheat to the river bank for winnowing. 'Why take it all the way over there?' asked helpful outsiders: 'Do it nearby.' So they did. A few years later, so the story went, the river bank collapsed and the area flooded. The chaff had been reinforcement.*

And another:

> *Motor vehicles, coal and the pesticide DDT were all once welcomed as 'solutions' to environmental problems. Then the solution became the problem (hat-tip Ed Conway).*

And another:

> *We'll give a bounty to anyone who kills a deadly snake and brings the head as proof, said the authorities in India. So people started breeding deadly snakes to cash in. Origin of the name 'Cobra effect'.*

In fact, this kickback – unwitting and usually unexpected (though not always) – includes a huge range of wicked complications that are described in smart-thinking under a mass of sometimes overlapping headings. Don't worry about the details, just feel the headaches:

- Unintended consequences
- The Cobra effect
- Feedback effects
- Compensatory effects
- Effects of effects, or secondary effects
- Externalities
- Collateral damage
- The tyranny of small decisions
- Moral hazard
- Short- versus long-term effects
- Perverse incentives
- The invisible foot (in contrast to the benign invisible hand referred to in economics)
- 'Seen' and 'unseen' consequences.[4]

Or, as I've seen it put: 'Getting Things Done IRL is Very Hard, Harder Than You Think' (IRL = in real life).[5] On top of this lot there's a whole bunch of strange effects that fall under the umbrella of complexity, such as policy resistance, when the world seems to have a will of its own that makes it impervious to the change we have in mind; non-linearity, when the relationship of what you put in and what you get out can go weird; or emergence, when the whole seems to be something entirely different in kind from the input of the parts.

If the jargon is strange, don't worry. We won't dwell on any of these (if you're curious, read the books). Anyway, we must move on. Because it's the explanation for problems like these that we're after. Which is? That life is made of systems.

This basic claim is timeless, and it's as the Buddha put it: 'Nothing ever exists entirely alone; everything is in relation to everything else.' In other words, life is complicated and, above all, connected, but our thinking often isn't. Our minds are set on the thing we want to accomplish. But pull on that thread, and you can't help pulling on a whole web of consequence.

The practical upshot is that when, with a gleam in our eye, we work out what'll work, we're casting a small pool of light in a large, dark room. We think we've seen everything relevant (what you see is all there is, WYSIATI, remember that?), but what's hiding in the shadows? Consequently, what we expect to happen doesn't.[6]

The point is to be sceptical whether 'I know what I'm doing and how to do it' can be relied on. In politics and business, 'I know what to do' is a condition of being taken seriously. You're someone with vision, with answers; you'll create the right incentives and that's it, sorted. But this talk is cheap, treating implementation of an idea like a mechanistic afterthought, like pulling a lever or winding a crank: 'Just get it done, why don't we?' Or: 'Let's just pass a law.'

So here are a couple of pictures to illustrate the contrast between the two models of thinking about how things might work out when we wind that crank. The first is a simple, mechanistic picture/metaphor for the way things are *supposed* to work, and often thought to work in a world of simple levers, a standard mousetrap: mouse grabs cheese, releases spring-loaded metal bar, no more mouse. Mission accomplished, as someone else said. If you get this wrong it's because you screwed up.

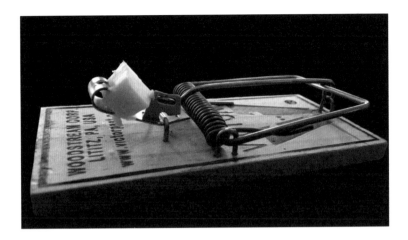

How it works 1.

In contrast, the *Mouse Trap* game – ever played? – was a Rube Goldberg-like contraption[7] that could, and did, go wrong every which way. Now why don't they describe policy like that, instead of saying it'll be sorted by Christmas?

When we try to pick up anything by itself we find it is attached to everything in the universe.

John Muir

How it works 2.

There's many a slip 'twixt cup and lip, as a poet once said. Or, as Gabriel Weinberg and Lauren McCann exaggerate in *Super Thinking*: 'Anything that can go wrong, will.' This mousetrap is the more iffy model to stick above the desk if you're thinking about social or political change, when you want a reminder that we live and work in systems.[8]

Honest question: which mousetrap is the more realistic model? Depends. How simple is your problem? How likely is it that something in the system will react in a way you hadn't anticipated? It's possible to exaggerate the risks of failure as well as the chance of success, so let's not presume one or the other. Overall, though, my sense is that we seem more over-confident than under-, hence the tone of this chapter. But, in the end, you make your own bet (see Chapter 12).

The world of systems is one where one act can have many consequences, but also where many factors shape one event. That's the web. And it's why controlling the parts is such a head-ache. 'Causes work in teams,' says the philosopher of science Nancy Cartwright,[9] and they do it every which way. So next, a picture I sometimes hand around to convey a little of this intri-cacy (I have a hard copy about a metre wide; people seem to like it). It shows a system with a few webs and threads, so far as we understand that system (NB: this is not a diagram, since I'll be amazed if you can extract any information from it; it's a picture of a diagram – different, so there). It's from Roche, a pharma company, and it's one of a pair. This one models metabolic pathways. I've marked and expanded a small section to give you a better sense of the detail. Haven't a clue what's going on in there. But I think of it whenever someone talks about a brilliant new nutritious wonderfood that works because... toxins... blah... gut bacteria... blah... blood type... brain food... something.

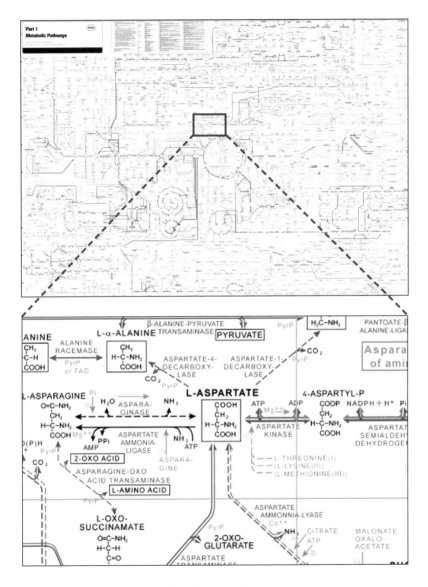

Details, details...

All you need do is work out how to change one little thing. Off you go! Spot a lever. Just don't mess with anything else. Looking at this, I almost think that if I do eat the nutri-bollocks wonderfood and it makes sod-all difference – which tends to be the case – I should think myself lucky.

I've picked up an annoying habit (only one?): when someone says, 'All we have to do is...', Roche's metabolic pathways come vaguely to mind. In a system, it's not easy to do 'all we need to do...' And after a while you suspect it's systems, and systems of systems, all the way down – not much that isn't in a web of some kind. 'Systems thinking', by the way, is a whole world of books on its own.[10] You might think from the way I've described it that it makes life hopeless, but it's not resigned in the face of complexity, and it would be wrong to characterize it as pessimistic. In fact it spends most of its time trying to find rules that govern complexity.

Overleaf, a few more systems: the coast (an ecosystem), snowflakes (every one unique, as you know, formed by complex physical systems), Pumpkin the dog (a system like any creature), a university (a social/educational system), the weather (part of the climate, an environmental system we worry we might have broken), a hospital (one part of a health and social-care system), a town lighting up at dusk (a power-generation and distribution system, among other things), and a few institutions. Is any of these systems less complicated than Roche's metabolic pathways?

I'm vaguely involved with a few of these systems and sometimes wonder: 'Why does it seem so complicated?' With the massive power of my hyper-rational intelligence, I've concluded: 'Maybe because it's complicated?' Sure, not all systems are equally elaborate – and how much we want to

mess with them also matters. Little answers to little problems in simpler systems tend to bring less kickback than big
answers to big problems (see Peter Sims' book *Little Bets*, for
the case for keeping your meddling small and incremental).
We could give Pumpkin the dog a trim without upsetting the
rest of her too much. We could change the BBC logo without
any material effect on anything, as companies do. We could
put a simple new bike chicane in that town there and...

Ach... nearly forgot. As we do. Even small tweaks can run
into complexity, they're just less likely to be the end of the
world. Thinking of change in isolation and ignoring all the
potential varieties of kickback is another of those intellectual
economies because we can't think of everything, but it might
leave us looking simple-minded. Secondary and system effects
are not the first thing on our mind. Nor should they be, often.
But if you act without thinking about them at all, you're not
thinking – you're wishful thinking.

*Since you're reading this book, you might have come
across the Trolley Problem. Do you divert a runaway
tram so that it avoids killing five people and kills only
one instead? It's become a famous, or maybe notorious, thought experiment. It's also absurdly simple.
As if you're ever in a situation when you know entirely
what the outcomes of a big intervention will be, and
these outcomes can be precisely specified, and they're
all the same kind (human lives lost), and so these pros
and cons are comparable and the practical difficulty
(switching a point) of choosing between them is practically trivial. Life isn't like that. But does that matter? Or
can this weird and crude simplification still help us*

think through more complex real-world problems? See Barbara Fried (see the note) for an argument for killing the Trolley Problem because it oversimplifies thinking about thinking.[11]

Do you look at that sorry chicane and wonder how 'install a chicane whenever a footpath is longer than X metres...' or whatever the policy was, came to this? How it failed to allow for local difficulties of execution? Strangely, everyone these days who studies policy failure groans about execution.[12] It's not only the what, they say, it's the detail of the how, and then the unsurprising surprise: 'Oh, wow, that turned out to be more complicated than we thought.'

One idea in this context is that 'context is king'. We met the same idea in one of the numbers chapters. Here, it means whatever rules, laws, principles, ideas you might think apply, it's context that decides if they work. Consequently know the landscape you're working in, know your context, is the frequent advice. But that can be harder than it sounds – because the problem with 'landscape' is that it gives the impression the context is stable, describable and, once known, predictable. Better, some say, to talk of a seascape, unstable and less predictable, where the world moves even as we observe it. So the problem is to make your idea work in a context like that. 'Seascape' is a fashionable metaphor among folk who talk about complexity.[13]

The policy landscape.

'The policy context is... now understood to be much more complex than had been previously recognized,' said recent research on how governments work, or don't. 'The factors that shape and influence implementation are seen to be complex, multifaceted and multileveled with public policies invariably resembling "wicked problems" that are resistant to change, have multiple possible causes, and with potential solutions that vary in place and time according to local context.'[14]

It's curious this line of argument should have caught on lately, when policy errors have been ten-a-penny for ever (see *The Blunders of Our Governments* by Ivor Crewe and Anthony King for twelve classic failures that blew a ton of cash and 'wrecked the lives of ordinary people'), and likewise examples of business miscalculation or overconfidence. It would be funny watching suits step in ditches, if we hadn't seen it so often. One line I like is that we should plan not on the basis that everyone carries out the plan as intended, but that there's a good chance someone, somewhere in the chain, will do it stupidly, or simply be unlucky.

I remember the radio presenter Evan Davies asking a government minster, 'What reasons did you consider why your policy might fail?' or something like that. No need to concede them, he said, just what were they. 'There aren't any,' she said, in so many words. 'What, none at all?' Evan asked – no way anything could possibly go wrong? Then he rattled off a couple of suggestions. Such is the game.

But this risk of glitch leaves a practical problem. Since it's hard to know if ideas will fly, whatever we think we know, then what? Do nothing? One answer is: be more adaptive. Whatever we try, be ready to try something else. Another strategy is that if it feels like you can't do anything without huge risk then, whenever possible, try before you fly. That is, experiment – preferably on a smaller scale than rolling out your shiny new idea across the whole country or business.

This takes us on a slightly different line of thought. But good experimental evidence from a well-designed study is as close to the real thing as there is and can help to reveal complications. Nothing new in this, but the principle is finally inching into government (see the 'Read on' section on page 295), growing bigger in social science (see the experimenters who won 2019 and 2021's Nobel Prizes for economics), standard in advertising and marketing (A/B testing, but see note[15]), etc. Experiment after a fashion is how machine learning works, by trying something – anything – and flinging a random solution at a problem that we know will be wrong initially, but learning from the feedback. Experiment, as Tim Harford points out, is how you turned out like you, via evolution (see also H. G. Wells: 'Biologically the species is the accumulation of the experiments of all its successful individuals since the beginning.'[16]). 'What's that?' you say. 'Is this guy finally endorsing a simple route to knowledge – namely, experiment?' Don't be daft.

Not so fast

Another awkward list...

1. Not every big policy problem exists in an unstable context like a seascape, or with uncertain outcomes like the chicane. Some problems have been there, unchanging, almost for ever, and we know the options and their likely outcomes, it's just that different people want different things, so we struggle to agree what to do. That's about politics and values more than systems.

2. All this experiment stuff... Yes, it's often revelatory, empirical research is top of my sources, but there's nothing simple about it and it's not enough. Experiments can be unreliable, falsified, hard to interpret, easy to do badly. Science is having that replication crisis that we heard about when many celebrated experiments failed to stand up. Even good experiments might not tell us all that they seem to.

   A political candidate asks a psychologist what TV ads to air in three contested districts. Luckily, the psychologist has new experimental research that, on average, people are more persuaded by attack ads than positive ads. The candidate is convinced – and loses by a landslide. Exit surveys blame the negative ads.

'In hindsight,' the psychologist explains 'the first district was probably too educated; I could see how attack ads might turn off highly educated voters. In the second, you have a lot of working-class who probably didn't like a female candidate publicly criticizing a male opponent. And in the third, I think the ads were just over-the-top. You want to highlight your opponent's flaws subtly, not make him sound like a cartoon villain.'

'OK, but why didn't you tell me these subtleties in advance?' the candidate asks.

'Well,' says the psychologist, 'the theory is true in general, but every situation is different.'

That little fiction is by Tal Yarkoni, a psychologist in Texas, who says psychology research – and by implication social science generally – is often less useful than claimed. Tightly defined, measurable experiments to prove an idea in the narrow context of the lab might not translate to the real, messy world where contexts vary – leading to the paradox that 'true in general' can be false almost every time. Not a case for giving up, maybe for calming down. Tal writes, 'If you choose to study extremely complex phenomena where any given behaviour is liable to be a product of an enormous variety of causal factors inter-acting in complicated ways, you probably shouldn't expect to be able to formulate clear law-like predictions capable of unambiguously elevating one explanation above others.'[17]

3. When the world's so messy, how do you isolate one bit to test? Which bit? How does it relate back to the whole?

It's been argued that the way rationality was tested in the 1970s, often by reducing it to one type of tightly defined test in a lab, meant we distorted the whole concept of rationality, and so mistook what smart-thinking should be in the first place (cue face-palm).[18] This means the smart-thinking tool we've just been celebrating – experiment – might have played a part in getting smart-thinking wrong. Irony overload or what?

4. You can't experiment with everything. In politics, an experimental Brexit wasn't on the table. Experiments also take time, and maybe you don't have any. Margaret Heffernan says experiment doesn't work in business, as everything keeps changing and the findings don't last (I disagree, but...). Experiment might also fall victim to the chicane problem: it misses how a chicane goes wrong in contexts that you didn't consider in the experiment. 'No, we didn't think to experiment next to a park.' There's an old line from psychologist Kurt Lewin: 'You can't understand a system until you try to change it.' Note, the 'it' he talks about changing is the system itself, the real world, not a proxy in a lab.

5. Good experiment might also need good theory, as experiment tells you what happens, but it doesn't really tell you *why* things happened, so the experiment can't be interpreted without causal assumptions – so be sure to do those properly, too.

   Once we say: a) we know only so much; and b) life is full of glitches and kickbacks, it's either experiment or gamble on what we think we already know (often both). The great caveat is that any experiment must be done well. Plenty aren't, and it's not unknown for the bad stuff to win most applause – the flashy, counter-intuitive findings that splash in the media or land in a Ted Talk. 'Ooh, real-life empirical evidence,' says an admiring crowd. But being an experiment alone isn't enough. Not even if it's done by a 'maverick' or heroic outsider, or because it's 'counter-intuitive' or new.

Bad experiment in a hurry by a maverick provoked zeal for an anti-malaria drug, hydroxychloroquine, as a remedy/prophylactic for Covid-19. Good experiment, by way of very large-scale randomized controlled trials, told us hydroxychloroquine was no good, but a steroid, dexamethasone, was the real deal. I'd bet on the difference with my life, which comes down to a bet on methodology. If I'm seriously sick with Covid-19, do not give me hydroxychloroquine. Do consider dexamethasone. But also bear in mind that there are such things as bad randomized trials (even good experimental methods can be abused).

I like experiment, like it so much I hate to see it done badly. Time invested understanding even the basics of good and bad experiment is priceless for thinking seriously about what works and what's true, in policy, medicine, business, you name it, but it's hard. It's also the exact opposite of giving up or doing nothing. Done well, it's the epitome of trying, then evaluating – and if the evidence says 'no', try something else. I like Emily Banks' formula: 'The only thing that truly works,' she says, is

> *evidence – implementation – action – evaluation – new evidence, round and round, for ever. A simpler version is: once you know it all, keep learning. At present the UK government evaluates about 8 per cent of its major projects. About the rest, presumably it knows it all already.*[19]

6. More generally on the ideas in this chapter... too much pessimism. You think anything ever got done by people accentuating every potential negative? Check out Hannah Ritchie's case for 'impatient optimism'.[20] This is another of those smart-thinking tensions: be sceptical, but also be optimistic.

7. You can be painfully aware of everything that could go wrong – and do it anyway, and that can be fine. Jeff Bezos thought the odds were stacked against Amazon. So did Elon Musk against Tesla. They didn't plan to fail, but expected to, and said it was still worth a try. So bad potential outcomes can be priced in and accepted (but bear in mind that we tend to be bad at pricing them accurately).

8. The problem with humility is that it can be close to defeatism. Is acknowledging complexity true humility or just a cover for bad attitude? Are we turning it into an excuse?

Pieces of story. *Rory's Story Cubes*
(no, I don't get commission).

11

Think twice
upon a time

Stories: love them and
mistrust them, both

O f all the ways of reasoning about what's going on out there, it's when I talk about it as storytelling that some audiences click.

Stories are everyday creative genius. They weave together facts, causes and feeling so that one thing leads seamlessly, persuasively to another, in fiction or non-fiction. A story can be a news story, your own life story, Shakespeare or a rom-com. Even an academic paper in the scientific journal *Nature* can take the form of a story. It's a powerful way of making sense of life, and some smart-thinkers will tell you that mastering storytelling is the secret to success. So this chapter is about thinking, and rethinking, in stories.

Because storytelling as thinking also gets us into trouble, and plenty of other smart-thinkers plaster it with warnings. So although simple narratives have a lot going for them – they might deliver an emotional hit, suggest a tidy causal path, have a neat conclusion and audiences might love them – the problem is (you've heard this before) *life is not like that*. So, if we do much of our thinking in stories (which we do), and we want to test our thinking (which we do), then a first trick has to be to rethink our stories. I'll try to describe what that involves by taking an example from the area I know best: journalism.

Journalists live and die by stories – that's what we in the trade call news reports. We think in stories and think of storytelling as key to the craft. We're not trying to write fiction – well, not all of us – because the first task is supposedly to work out what's really going on out there. But the idea of a story shapes our thinking from the off. In other words, journalists approach evidence much like everyone else, by thinking about how it fits into a story.

How does this work out? Often great, sometimes... not.

The following is a little parodied from my days as a hack, but recognizable. Crudely, we went about describing the world by building a narrative arc – a story – from a standard kit of parts consisting of the supposed elements of knowing, while also trying to grab your attention. It went a little like this...

1. Here's Andrew. A terrible thing happened to poor Andrew, we said, trying to pull you in by the heart. (This part is the anecdote, though we didn't call it that, we called it 'the human interest', and sometimes 'the case study'.)

2. Andrew is 'just the tip of the iceberg', we said, almost as a rule – leading the audience via his fate to some ideally shocking numbers about the extent of problems like his, which are of course Facts. (This part we called 'the evidence'.)

3. So let Andrew be a lesson. And here is that lesson, because next come experts to explain how and why it all happened. (This part we might call 'context'.)

4. Then, because we're at a critical point in our narrative arc, some conflict – as conflict is good in a story
   (though we didn't call it that, we called this part
   'balance'). So here's a politician or campaigner who
   is outraged at what happened to Andrew and has an
   easy answer, plus someone from the other side with
   another.

5. And finally here's what they do about it in Scandinavia,
   which works blissfully, so let's roll that out across the
   country and live happily ever after.

Parodied, but not far off. Those are the story elements, and
don't they roll together nicely as one follows the other? Once
on this train, it can be hard to get off. It all seems so neat, so
true, so complete.

How does it go wrong? Let's add some flesh and blood to
make it a real example.

This was the story of Andrew Marr, a well-known journalist and TV presenter who had a stroke in middle age. It was
genuinely shocking – and just the tip of the iceberg. Hospitals
were treating many more strokes among the middle-aged: up
a massive 46 per cent in fifteen years for men aged forty to
fifty-four. These were the facts and the evidence. 'The Stroke
Association described the increase as alarming,' said one
national newspaper, 'a sad indictment of the nation's health.'
These were the experts with the context, which was all to do
with rising obesity. Then came various people to say what
must be done.

This is a blend of several prominent news stories and features at that time, all real. Never mind that Andrew Marr was

one of the thinnest, fittest fifty-somethings going; 'if it could happen to him it could happen to anyone.' Strokes are up and you – yes, you, middle-aged man with the burger – are in peril.[1]

Again, all effortlessly believable. And true – in parts. And nothing wrong with encouraging healthy living, or with the reality of Andrew's experience. So what's wrong with the story?

Have a think while we take a detour.

When I trained journos at the BBC, we set them this task: explain why shark attacks and ice-cream sales rise and fall together.

We weren't especially looking for the real answer (but go ahead). The aim was other, weirder answers, to be creative and restless about how one thing leads to another. Why crazy answers?

Two reasons. First, because too often we allow our story-telling instincts to stop too soon. We let them settle on the first story that makes a sense that we like. But writing the story, and rewriting the story, draws on the same imaginative capacity. All you have to do is keep going. And we wanted journos in the habit of not stopping; to stay restless about how the story fits together, and to learn to enjoy the feeling of coming up with alternatives.

Second, we wanted to show how bad stories can still make a kind of sense, so people could see why they might *need* to keep going. So they had sixty seconds to think of the best alternative stories they could for the sharks–ice-cream link.

A couple of answers from over the years: 'Warmer weather brings people to beaches, people buy ice-cream at beach, sharks see ice-cream, sharks become jealous. The sharks will stop at nothing for a 99 with a flake.'

And my all-time favourite… 'What you don't realize is it's easier to swim away from a shark if you are not trying to hold on to an ice-cream.'

Which is just delicious, because it has a strange plausibility, don't you think? Do you know what I mean? It sort of makes sense. You're out on the blue, floating serenely, Cornetto in hand, when the *Jaws* theme kicks in. You betcha your freestyle is cramped.

If something so absurd has even the tiniest scrap of narrative plausibility, it hints at what makes stories so dangerous. They can carry you from evidence through fragments of reason, all the way to tempting plausibility on a stream of bullshit. Everything that makes stories compelling can be a source of con.

So what do we do? Luckily, the creative connections that sweep us to belief also hint at our way out. With stories, we either let the plausibility take us or we exploit our capacity to tell *and retell*. That is, take the story elements – like the shark and the ice-cream – and break them apart. Then start playing with the pieces. It's the plausible cohesion of narrative that makes it so dangerous, so the skill is to tear it up. 'Unpack the components,' say Philip Tetlock and Dan Gardner in *Superforecasting*.

Separate the pieces into pictures – like the pictures in this chapter of ice-creams and sharks. Evaluate the parts and their connections. Add more elements that could be relevant. Play around with them. See how else they can be stuck together. Anything to resist the strange magic of the story that binds a few chosen pieces into one settled narrative. If you can create a story from them once, you can pull it to bits and start again, differently, and you can enjoy it.

By the way, if you're struggling with the sharks–ice-creams, the answer to what sticks them together is summer: summer = more ice-cream sales, summer = more swimming, and more swimming = more shark attacks.

The point of these games is to become rapid hypothesis-generating machines – to spin off stories (plural) using the material creatively, without the craving to settle too quickly on one story we like. And in case you feel game-playing is beneath you, it's not only a game; the best analytical brains around aspire to it.

Here's Cassie Kozyrkov, chief decision scientist at Google:

> Expert analysts never try to sell you a story found by torturing data until it confesses. Instead, they use hedging/softening language when talking about their findings and they have the discipline to come up with multiple interpretations for *everything*. If you suspect someone is an analytics Jedi, try this trick: ask them to interpret some data/graph for you. The faster they produce multiple explanations and the more alternatives they generate, the more the force is with them. If they get stuck on just one explanation, they're still in their larval amateur phase.

If you want to be an analytics Jedi and practise the multi-story generating skill without going near data, you can cultivate your story instincts and enjoy telling and retelling with the children's game *Story Cubes*.

Story cubes are dice with images instead of numbers, like an arrow →, a bee 🐝, a hand ✋, a plane ✈, a world 🌍, a fire 🔥. The rules are simple: roll the dice, tell a story.

Struck by Cupid's arrow →
but stung 🐝
by rejection ✋
I travelled ✈
far away 🌍
where in bitterness I became a pyromaniac 🔥.

Easy. It's a measure of our gift for constructing narrative, but also worrying: the same ability to find sense goes hand-in-hand with the ability to string together stories from any old crap.

When people are truly terrible at forecasting – which we are – but find explanations for history relatively easy, the difference, sceptics say, is because we're doing a story-cube job on the past. We don't really know as well as we think we do why things happened as they did, but we do know how to arrange the pieces to tell a plausible story, once the dice have rolled. People are brilliant at fitting the pieces together. But the satisfaction of putting the dice in order doesn't tell us the arrangement is true.

Luckily, as we say, the problem can be part of the solution. If imagination can get us into this, maybe it can get us out, or at least test the story we've already told – by rearranging our cubes. We can use stories to challenge stories.

Struck by Cupid's arrow →
but rejected ✋
I embraced nature 🐝
and vowed to save the world 🌍
from climate change 🔥
so caught the next plane ✈.

If you want to give story cubes a go, try a variation on the standard game which we'll call 'flash story cubes'. Roll three cubes once — only once, don't touch them again — and see how many different stories you can tell in one minute. Give your creative retelling a workout.

My own sceptical take is that a lot of thinking is about as robust as playing story cubes: putting together bits of evidence that vaguely hang together, then feeling satisfied. But the intuition we gain from playing the game is that satisfying arrangements are easy; true ones more elusive. But at least we can learn to replay.

That's the analogy. How does this work when we're not playing a game? Back to our story about Andrew Marr and the huge rise in strokes. Take two elements from that story with some sort of link, two story cubes:

- Strokes
- Hospitals

Maybe we think: 'There's only one way to join these, one story. Strokes and hospitals go together.' If we do, we're normal. But we've just drawn a flying unicorn — come to a fast and intuitive conclusion about what the evidence means that seems to have internal logic. The BBC did this and reported more strokes, because hospital data for strokes was up.

How about rethinking the story? This time work out why fewer people might be having strokes, despite what the hospital numbers say. Think of a different relationship between strokes and hospitals. Note, this is not numeracy — it's imagination. What else could be going on to explain that rise in people treated?

Not everyone finds this easy, so here's a clue: 'hospitals *treat* more strokes'. That is, the number of strokes and the number treated in hospitals ain't necessarily the same thing. Still puzzled? OK, not all strokes end up in hospital.

To spell that out, not so long ago a lot of people who had strokes were sent home by their GP and told to lay off the booze and rest. Now they go to hospital ASAP, aware they need treatment fast. They're also more aware when they've had one. So it's not strokes that are up, it's how often people get hospital care when it happens. That's what's going up. According to the limited evidence of stroke incidence in the whole population, strokes were most likely sharply down in this period, because smoking was – the stories were 180 degrees wrong on this. There's some suggestion that the average age of first stroke might have lowered slightly, but this may be because we know about cases that previously went under the radar. Overall, the whopping rise reported in the media wasn't credible.[2]

When I ask what this other story could be, faces leave the room for a minute, then a few come back with a smile and the answer. Until prompted, hardly any think to wonder. So it's not the difficulty, it's recognizing the need to get off our one-story-will-do arse when that story is plausibly, persuasively stuck together. Plausible, clearly, doesn't mean true. Plausibility, in fact, can either be a clue or it can be a con, by acting like a cognitive anaesthetic. Don't succumb too soon. Stay restless. Pull the story pieces apart. Reimagine them. The experimental psychologist Gary Klein defines insight as a 'shifting of stories'.[3]

Careful, though. It's true there's a link between obesity and strokes, just that it wasn't strong enough to outweigh less smoking. Nonsense often contains sense – that's why we break up the whole to test the parts. But don't expect to break things conclusively every time. The first story will often be the right one. Be willing to test it, that's all, as the same evidence (or, if you're a wannabe data Jedi, the same data) can be consistent with wildly different stories.

Evidence/story? Tell the story of the top picture. Then enjoy the second picture as an imaginative suggestion. Though how this bike is meant to work... (see Chapter 8). Credit: Dr. Whiger (via: http://twitter.com/drwhiger).

Or here's one for the techies. The images below are known as the Datasaurus Dozen – twelve charts, plus one joke dinosaur. They are all, as you see, very different. Except they're not. Because in one sense the story they tell is exactly the same. The mean of the position of every dot or data point on the X-axis is the same, to two decimal places. Ditto the Y-axis. A measure of how spread out the dots are – the standard deviation, often used in statistics – is the same. ('Corr.' means Pearson's correlation – look it up). So you could say that all thirteen pics, including the dinosaur, can be summarized with just one story. Now imagine that exercise backwards. You have one data story: how many variations of evidence could be consistent with it?

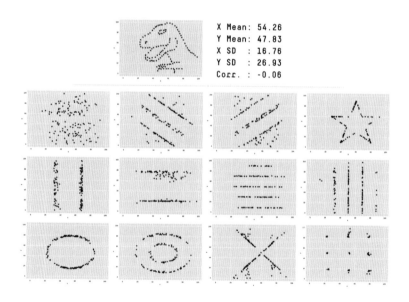

The **Datasaurus Dozen**, plus dinosaur.[4]

If it weren't that I didn't want to fill this book with diagrams, I'd have used a whole load of screen-grabs here from an animation that shows a bunch of moving dots, then superimposes the slowly rotating triangles that these dots represent. The triangles can be seen like the bigger story, based on the evidence.

Except that you can also impose moving squares on exactly the same pattern of dots, and they rotate in the opposite direction – a completely different story using identical evidence. Or you can impose one large, slowly rotating star. Or all three shapes at once, in some weird, shifting 3D polyhedron. They all fit the same pattern of moving dots. It's a sublime visualization of 'model equivalence' or 'underdetermination' – when the evidence doesn't wholly determine the beliefs we hold about it and can be compatible with very different interpretations. To see this visualization and be amazed, follow the endnote. Never again will you assume you know what story the evidence implies. Well, you will, but you might be more careful.[5]

One of the biggest elements of a story is causality. This is what tells us how one thing leads to another. Causality in narrative is a mammoth subject, but they all are, so let's dive in.

As the novelist E. M. Forster almost said: 'The King died, the Queen died' is nothing to 'the King died, then the Queen died of grief.' It's not only the what, it's the why. Causation is the why, the glue that holds a story together.

But this is glue that needs pulling apart. Back to our example again, and we can see how the casual claim creeps in: it's true that middle-aged men can have strokes, look at Andrew Marr; it's true that more middle-aged men are going to hospital with strokes, look at the data; it's true that obesity makes a stroke more likely and we know there's more obesity. And, before you know it, you've bought the casual claim that obesity is leading directly to a whopping rise in strokes.

This is a heap of evidence, knowledge and belief – often emotion, too – all bound together by causation into just about the biggest unit of evidence there is, the story. That's part of its power. It pulls everything together; everything seems to support our explanation. That's why de-composing the story is one of the best ways to test it. To rethink evidence, especially about causes, we need to pull apart the story elements. Step back, look at them coldly, separately.[6]

Some social scientists like to do this explicitly with their causal assumptions – we're into lofty academic territory here – with causal diagrams called DAGs, directed acyclic graphs. (Again, look them up.) Forget the jargon, mull the principle – pictures. Well, arrows, anyway, to lay out a causal story. Such as...

screen time ⟶ obesity

Clear enough what that means? Or maybe it needs teasing out...

screen time ⟶ physical activity ⟶ obesity

That is, it's not a direct cause, it's mediated. Thinking about and drawing out mediating parts of the story helps. Thinking about what the arrows mean helps, too. How *exactly* does physical activity relate to obesity?

But what if...

parental behaviour/education

screen time ⟶ physical activity ⟶ obesity

When maybe the 'screen time ⟶ obesity' explanation isn't straightforward, and parents are the common cause of both, with multiple upbringing failures (parents – I'm one of them – are usually to blame). Or maybe it's like this:

screen time ⟵ physical activity ⟵ obesity

And the arrows point the other way, so obesity causes less physical activity. And so on.[7]

I'm not saying these are the answers, let alone all of them. The technique helps us reflect, that's all, on what can otherwise slide past through story and assumption into comfy explanation. It helps us rethink, helps look for errors. Some researchers swear by it, though it seems to me better at clarifying problems with our causal stories than at giving definitive answers. But that's still a help. Maybe next time you're puzzling over a story, draw it.

And by the way, ever noticed that most smart-thinking books take the form first of a story, then a claim that this story demonstrates some big causal claim, followed by heaps of data and science? 'It was a June day in Nebraska when... which just goes to show how.... as proved by stunning research published in...' It's the ABC of pop science. If you want to rethink smart-thinking, rip apart its stories.[8]

Stories satisfy our sense of order. They feel complete, without loose ends, and this feeling that everything fits, that it's all coherent, reassures us that we know the truth. So remember how easily we can knock up a coherent story after the dice have rolled, and that 'easy', 'satisfying', 'coherent' and 'plausible' don't equal 'true'.

Not so fast

A pile of reasons to be careful...

1. You can have too much of a good thing. Overdo the creative imagination for stories and we're back with the unicorns of wild conspiracy theory. So, once we've dreamed up alternative stories, the job is nowhere near done. All we have is a bunch of rival explanations. Next, we need to evaluate these explanations.

   This difference between explaining and evaluating is easily confused, says David Lagnado in *Explaining the Evidence*. Think of crime. 'The accused did it because he needed money...' That's a plausible story/explanation, but it's not an evaluation. The evaluation is when we ask how good this explanation is. In other words, is it the right one? David thinks we're good at explaining, not good at evaluating. So once we've done the creative part and come up with alternative stories, we start judging: which story is the best fit? And that is a whole world of difficulty. The ability to challenge a story is a tiny part of finding the right one.

2. We've heard reasons to suspect stories – journalists suckered by the flow of evidence – but somehow, in the end, we must still synthesize that evidence. Stories remain the great synthesizers: instinctive, efficient mental models of how life is causally arranged. Add emotion, names and faces for a human connection, a touch of satisfying detail here and there, and a direction to the story with a beginning and end and they're almost irresistible – and engaging people matters. In the end, whatever storytelling's dangers, we still tell a story. Extra reason to make it the right one.

   Likewise, casual reasoning keeps us alive and functioning. So before writing us off, tip a hat to how our tools of understanding are fabulously adapted to help us get by. The trick is to see that this everyday genius can go to work on junk, and to bear that in mind, keep our conclusions provisional and be as willing as we can to rewrite the story. Also remember how far our own causal competence runs. The answer, usually, is not far (see Chapter 8, 'Draw the tiger'). Overall, it's a fine balance between the brilliance and utility of stories and their treachery. As usual, no one perspective tells you what to do.

3. We build belief and opinion with many bricks, one on top of another. To rethink just one brick (one piece of the story) can involve shaking the whole thing. This is a big deterrent. Easier sometimes to live in a semi-ruin. (For more on this, look up 'belief perseverance'.)

4. Another word about opening our minds to alterative stories. So that I stay open-minded to other potential

stories, can someone find me a Nazi to talk to? (NB: major sarcasm alert.) There's a saying: 'Don't be so open-minded your brains fall out.'[9] In other words, everything has limits. So, obvious problem: what are the limits to opening your mind to alternative stories – aside from the dangers of smugness and complacency – and how do you know you've hit them? Am I obliged to open my mind to people who are plainly clueless, or if I suspect they're acting in bad faith? Worse, since there are always exceptions to taking other people's stories seriously, anyone can abuse that to justify their own take: 'Oh, sure, people need to be open-minded, platitude, platitude... but in this case I don't have to listen to you because you're evil' and then defend their rigidity as principle or common sense, while dissing other people's open minds as naivety: 'You're not open-minded, you're a sucker.'

For now, let's stick with the threats from you to your own thinking. Too much of an open mind is seldom one of them, and my guess is that you – like all of us – can open yours to a little more imaginative rethinking.

Let's end on creativity. Here's François Jacob, a Nobel-winning biologist, who talked about 'night science' – a gorgeous metaphor for the thinking that never makes it into the formal 'day science' of experiment, the scientific journal or the news, the restless background instinct that rips things up and imagines:

'Night science wanders blind. It hesitates, stumbles, recoils, sweats, wakes with a start. Doubting everything, it is forever trying to find itself, question itself, pull itself back together. Night science is a sort of workshop of the possible where what will become the building material of science is worked out... Where phenomena are still mere solitary events with no link between them.' [12]

It's all part of the routine, folks.

Try this

There are people I know whose reflex is to pull apart causal explanations. For them, it's like an itch. They buzz with alternative stories, like rapid hypothesis-generating machines. Many of these people, curiously, are statisticians, inviting the terrible thought that a bunch of number-nerds might have a better imagination for the backstory than me, an English grad. The shame! But can the rest of us learn from them and make this a habit? We can try. Start with some non-political examples and try pulling these stories apart and retelling them, as many ways as you can, by explaining why...

1. Compared to families with no babies, on the rooftops of homes with a baby you're more likely to find a stork.

2. People who take vitamin E live longer.

Then try a seriously sensitive example. First, identify the story you'd like to tell, then pull it apart. Again, we're after a harvest of ideas, not a conclusion.

3. There's more crime where migrants live.

And then another incendiary one, which might even be true. But don't decide, just enjoy testing it to pieces. Feel your passion rise as you read it, then breathe, and tell the emotion to get lost while you tell stories (plural), calmly, ruthlessly, every which way. Remember, this is a test of imagination.

4. Boomers cornered all the money.

Explanations can be serious or ridiculous, doesn't matter. The main thing is to make a creative act of testing and retesting your first thoughts. Flex your causality muscles — and don't be tempted to stop as soon as you feel comfortable. Any fool can do that, and everyone does. Especially don't stop with the story you like best. In fact, work out what you want the story to be, and question evidence in its favour harder than you question the alternatives, to fight your self-serving instincts. And by the way, it doesn't count as creative to grab at conspiracy theories or 'people are just lying' as your alternative stories. People do lie, of course they do, but if those are all the stories you have, I'm already bored.

The whole idea is that instead of closing a story down, fixing it with one interpretation, we're opening it up, to see it in different ways, to resist what's been called 'the rage to conclude'[10] and instead let imagination show us other possibilities. So many of the brains we turn to in public argument seem to rage towards the same story every time. If they read this book, it would confirm everything they already knew. Don't be one of those people. They've already died.

Try this

One to play with: what's going on in the picture of the guys and the truck? Identify all the elements of cause and correlation that do, do not or might explain the scene. Imagination, please. Enjoy yourself, maybe tell a few stories and nurture your sense that the right to say 'because' is hard-earned. The picture became a small-scale internet meme in 2021. Suggestions below.

You need a story to displace a story.

Nassim Taleb

Tell me a story. Identify causes and correlations.

With that, we can go back to our pictures of the shark, the beach and the ice-cream, or our strokes and hospitals, and think about the elements, and the arrows and mediating factors, and play with the pieces, creatively.

One piece of any story is especially worth a rethink: the desire to put us – people – at its centre, as if visible human action is always the thing what dunnit. Here's David Spiegelhalter, who wrote *The Art of Statistics*:

> *Just because we act, and something changes, it doesn't mean we were responsible for the result. Humans seem to find this simple truth difficult to grasp – we are always keen to construct an explanatory narrative, and even keener if we are at its centre. Of course sometimes this interpretation is true – if you flick a switch, and the light comes on, then you are usually responsible. But sometimes your actions are clearly not responsible for an outcome: if you don't take an umbrella, and it rains, it is not your fault.*[11]

Jargon

- *Seize and freeze*: a psychology term for instinctively grasping at a quick answer or explanation, then holding tight.[13]

- *Pernicious rationalization*: overdoing our storytelling by using high intelligence to create explanations and connections, unaware that such cleverness can work against us.

- *Causality illusion*: too easily assuming one thing causes another.

- *Paltering*: a word that smart-thinkers like. It means using small truths to convince people of a big untruth, which is how bad stories often work.

The truck

- It's obvious, the guy is reversing – that's why he's looking behind. The others are trying to stop him.
- No, seriously, it was a breakdown. Obviously.
- And, clearly, three pushing, one pretending (correlation not causation by the pretender).
- Or maybe one pushing, three pretending?
- Although since they were nearly nicked for parking, maybe they're all pretending that it was a breakdown.
- But was it a breakdown or did they run out of fuel? And how come they ran out of fuel (how far back do you have to go to explain causes)?
- They're scarcely pushing at all, any of them; it's rolling downhill (I tilted the picture, but let's pretend). Or maybe...

A short story about decisions.
Originally by Limehelmet on Reddit.

12

Think in bets

Make peace with uncertainty

Y ou're a cat in Austin, Texas, and you can guess what it's probably like outside – a range of scenarios anyway – from experience only of course, because no one talks to you much about the weather: you're the cat. Anyhow the sky looks clear from the sofa, so time for a wander.

So you let the guy know in the usual way and he opens the door. And weird... white stuff – do I remember this? Maybe just one little... And, hey, what the...! Cancel everything. New information.

A story in a picture, and more than a story. Welcome to what I'm going to call Bayesian thinking[1] – and thereby probably annoy a few people. Little does the cat know it could be a practitioner. It's left such crisp evidence of what was going on in its little cat brain that we'll make it the poster cat for a big theme in smart-thinking; to some, a whole philosophy.

Read the books and eventually you'll come across it. Or maybe 'Bayes' and 'Bayesian' have popped onto your radar, but never looked tempting. If you've ever wondered or struggled, but didn't get round to finding out, here's half the answer in an image. Doesn't look like this in the books – more likely you'll see an equation – but this is roughly what it is, only less formal, by a cat.

The simplest definition I've seen of Bayesian thinking goes a little like this: start with what you believe given your evidence, add more, see where you get. Doesn't sound too radical, does it? In fact is this just a fancy way of talking about changing your mind? Almost, but stick with us for a minute or two.

Bayes theorem dates from the eighteenth century when a Nonconformist minister, the Revd Thomas Bayes, had an idea that waited about 250 years to become big – and maybe changed a little from what he had in mind – which we can also put like this: what we think is up is only what we *think* with a certain degree of confidence, given the evidence we have, and we update this belief with new information. The principle is so core to some people's thinking that they call themselves Bayesians. I'm a bit that way myself (though there are chunks of Bayesian statistics that are beyond me).

Or as Wiki puts it: 'The theorem expresses how a degree of belief, expressed as a probability, should rationally change to account for the availability of related evidence.'

Applied to the cat, we see a degree of belief in the prospect of a wander, conditional on a clear sky, rationally changed to account for the evidence of a cold paw. Bayesian thinking is said to be a good fit for human intuition, too.

You can if you want, as Wiki implies, put a number on your initial degree of belief – 'What's the probability of this thing?' (in this case a wander, given a clear sky), then put a number on the value of any new evidence, and calculate how one changes the other so that you go from a prior to a posterior belief, to use the jargon. That's where the equation comes in (feel free to look it up). If you really want, you can flounce around talking about your 'priors', if you don't mind ridicule; or you can spend a lifetime learning the finer points of Bayesian statistics and have huge rows with different flavours of statistician and others. But the basic idea needs none of that. The 'Bayesian brain', as it's been called, is like the cat: we form beliefs about or expectations of our environment, given certain evidence, and then, if we're paying attention, we note unexpected features to recalibrate.

OK, but if a cat does it, what's the big deal? Well, now...

First, let's get serious about what 'degree of belief' means. Any degree of belief short of cast-iron certainty also means a degree of doubt. OK then, face that degree of doubt. State it, even quantify it — how sure/unsure are you, exactly? This is quite the refocus when we do so love to emphasize the knowing part and ignore the rest. Rebalancing attention from what we know, towards what we don't know, changes how we see the world.

Steven Pinker says: 'Probabilities are not about the world; they're about our *ignorance* of the world.'[2] Well, both, I'd say. But ignorance is in there and we should face it squarely.

Next (and this is where it's weird), this applies not only to what's most obviously hard to know with certainty: the future; it also applies here and now, to present facts. The snow has fallen, its existence is a fact, but are you sure of it and its effect on your wander?[3]

Put those together and we get a little radical: it means we can have a degree of uncertain belief in facts. Wait — a what? How do you have a *degree* of *belief* in facts? Facts are 100 per cent facts, aren't they?

If you've not thought like this before, cogs may be grinding, so let's walk it through.

I'm about to flip a fair coin — the result is still in the future — and the chance of heads is, what, 50:50?

I flip the coin, but hide the result. What's the chance of heads now (the result is no longer in the future, it's now a fact)? You don't know, and so you might still say 50:50.

But it's a fact.

Yep, but so far as you're concerned, still 50:50.

So a present fact can be only a probability?

Guess so, because it's not yet fully present to you. It's conditional on what you know.

Next I look at the coin, but keep it hidden from you. Now what's the chance of heads? Still 50:50 for you, maybe; but for me zero, because I know, but I'm not telling that it landed tails. Now you and I have different degrees of belief in the facts. You think 50:50, I think zero. In other words, our relationship to facts is subjective. What we think depends on what's in our heads – yours and mine – and it can differ; it's not always a property of the coin, it's not a given.[4]

Use a word like 'subjective' around facts and someone will accuse you of arguing that facts are whatever you want them to be. So let's stamp on that. If we both look and we're sober, and it's heads, then it's heads. You cannot call it tails. Well, you can, but I'll be edging for the door. Subjectivity is bounded by evidence, clearly; it's not limitless. In this case, the subjectivity goes only so far as there's uncertainty. Even so, belief is what we're often left with, even when it's about a fact, because the evidence is seldom complete and so we must judge what we can believe, given what we've got. If we're honest, most of the 'what's up?' questions that interest us in life have degrees of belief and of uncertainty.[5]

Still with us? Fab, you could be a Bayesian. But we're not done, because all this changes you. Working out what's up becomes less a quest for certainties, less about labelling once and for all what's black or white, true or false, in a way that's somehow objective and out there; more about the uncertain, conditional in-betweens, the changing shades of grey – so far as we can know them: 'Degree, not absolute. A needle moving across not an on–off switch,' said one smart dude.[6] This is a very particular way of thinking about almost everything.

Sure, you can insist, if you like, that even if you don't know thing X with certainty, you still know enough. This might be fine if the question is whether the parrot nailed to the perch is dead, an ex-parrot;[7] maybe not so fine on Saddam Hussein's weapons of mass destruction. We need ruthless realism about our uncertainties.

With that, we can savour a few implications. First, that it can be wise to hold back before saying 'we know' and bounding into the snow, unless we've also calibrated our uncertainty and we're happy with it. I've even seen it said that reserving judgement like this is the essence of critical thinking. Next, we could be less defensive about being hedgy, less apologetic about making modest bets, and simply accept that's how life is, even though this means sharing our ignorance.

My advice is that if you don't know, say so. It's not an 'admission' – it is what it is. Doesn't mean we go uncertainty-crazy and say, 'Ugh, no one can know anything, so let's give up, go back and curl up on the sofa with the cat.' All it means is we accept that knowledge is not often 100 per cent, but it's not often zero, either. We say what kind of grey this is, darker or lighter, and what makes us think so.

As the legendary statistician David Spiegelhalter put it: 'In a world in which strident voices dominate, open acknowledgment of what we don't know could be a very small step to humility and trustworthiness. Of course, just because we don't know everything doesn't mean we don't know anything... We should be clear on what we do know and proclaim our uncertainty with confidence.'[8]

Note: 'proclaim' our uncertainty, not 'admit'. There's no shame here. If you're in the habit of 'admitting' uncertainty, stop, and start proclaiming it instead.

'Proclaim uncertainty with confidence' is a deliberate paradox (or is it technically an aporia? not sure). If there's one thing we can (probably) say for sure, it's that there's much to be unsure about. A repeated theme of smart-thinking – and perhaps the biggest theme of this book – is learn to love uncertainty. Or, if loving goes too far, at least make peace with it. People are said to hate uncertainty, but if that means we scramble for unjustified certainties, it's not thinking, it's more wishful thinking.

All fine and dandy, if hard to swallow for some. But... is it true? Is uncertainty really the best strategy? Are you sure (that's a joke)? What's the evidence that uncertainty pays off? In *Zero Dark Thirty*, the film of the raid that killed Osama bin Laden, the hero is sure bin Laden is in the compound. 'He's there, 100 per cent,' she says. All the uncertain others are a faffy waste of space, we're given to understand. Heroes know, and the climactic scene proves who the heroes are. Political leaders likewise know – or think they do – not to offer voters a flip-flopping, fence-sitting, mid-range percentage or probability.

But against that, here are a few smart-thinkers who bet heavily on shades of grey – and win...

> *Annie Duke – isn't that a great name, a gunslinger name? – is a former pro poker player who won more than $4 million. Then she wrote* Thinking in Bets. *Read it: it's clear, thoughtful, clever, a joy. In poker, she says, she had*

to put her money where her thinking was; there was no
room for illusions if she wanted to come out ahead.

'A hand of poker takes about two minutes. Over the
course of that hand, I could be involved in up to twenty
decisions. And each hand ends with a concrete result: I
win money or I lose money.'

So if her thinking wasn't productive, she changed
it. Top of her list of failed thoughts? 'Black and white
thinking' (variously described by others as 'dichotomous
thinking'/'binary thinking'/'the tyranny of the discon-
tinuous mind'). Black-and-white thinking sees the world
divided into two possibilities: one right, one wrong. You
play a hand, you win, you were right. You lose, you were
wrong. Right? Wrong. What poker taught her, Annie says,
is that we live in a wide, foggy zone in between, which at
the time of the decision is neither black nor white, neither
right nor wrong. The best poker players and decision-
makers know this and act/bet on it, sensitive to the
probabilities and uncertainties. She says:

> *There are many reasons why wrapping our arms*
> *around uncertainty and giving it a big hug will help us*
> *become better decision-makers. Here are two of them.*
> *First, 'I'm not sure' is simply a more accurate repre-*
> *sentation of the world. Second, and related, when we*
> *accept that we can't be sure, we are less likely to fall*
> *into the trap of black-and-white thinking...*
>
> *If we misrepresent the world at the extremes of*
> *right and wrong, with no shades of grey in between,*
> *our ability to make good choices – choices about how*
> *we are supposed to be allocating our resources, what*

> kind of decisions we are supposed to be making, and
> what kind of actions we are supposed to be taking –
> will suffer. The secret is to make peace with walking
> around in a world where we recognize that we are not
> sure and that's okay.[9]

Annie Duke's biggest lesson? Shun black-and-white think-ing, cease treating every win as vindication and every loss as failure, stop looking for easy meanings like that, because often they just weren't there when it mattered. Instead, accept that any outcome is a mixture of both judgement and luck. If we bet on odds 90:10 in our favour, but lose, blame misses the point. The 10 was always possible, and the fact it showed up was bad luck. It tells you nothing more than that. Likewise, winning lucky teaches us nothing about the quality of our decision, no matter how good winning might feel.

Annie says: 'What makes a decision great is not that it has a great outcome. A great decision is the result of a good process, and that process must include an attempt to accurately repre-sent our own state of knowledge. That state of knowledge, in turn, is some variation of "I'm not sure."'

Treating outcomes as if they're judge and jury of all we do – a habit that pro poker players refer to with a sneer as 'resulting' – ignores life's uncertainties, pretends luck doesn't exist, twists bad decisions that luck-out into good decisions, and vice versa, so it learns the wrong lessons from experience.

To win not once but often, Annie redefined right and wrong not by how things turned out, but according to cold-hearted probabilities at the moment of decision. Even 99:1 in your favour still gives the 1 a chance. If it wins, the 99 was still best, given what you knew.

If that strikes you as crazy, if your instinct is 'How could it be right when it turned out wrong?' – if you think you smell a loser's excuses – remember that Annie won millions, and ditto every other great poker player. 'Wanna bet?' she says. You bet on your thinking, she'll bet on hers. I bet Annie beats you.

As she says, we need to stop treating 'I don't know' and 'I'm not sure' like strings of dirty words. 'All bets are only as good as our beliefs,' she says, like a good Bayesian – even though she never uses the word – adding: 'Part of the *skill* in life comes from learning to be a better belief calibrator.' And that's what this is all about: belief calibration.

Couldn't say precisely how much of Annie's advice the cat absorbed, as the cat and I haven't discussed it. If that paw was tentative and not a rush of self-confidence, by my reckoning that's a 76 per cent Bayesian cat that sensibly recalibrated. I'm ready to revise that on more evidence, naturally.

So we have two parts to Bayes. First, that knowledge is about degrees of belief; second, linked to the first, it's learning from experience or new information to update by degrees. But the bottom line is, it's all degrees; we live in uncertainty.

I promised more cheerleaders for this view. Here's the second: Philip Tetlock and Dan Gardner's superforecasters.

> *Like Annie Duke, superforecasters win. They take part in forecasting competitions and play on the turn-up not of cards, but of real-world 'high-stakes' events, forecasting between three and eighteen months out. Superforecasters beat subject specialists, the intelligence community, everyone. How? In many ways the same as poker players – they're intuitive Bayesians.*

> *Philip and Dan write: 'What matters more to the superforecasters than Bayes theorem is Bayes core insight of getting closer to the truth by constantly updating in proportion to the evidence.' These updates tend to be small, moving incrementally from an initial estimate as new information comes in. 'Units of doubt', they call them.*
>
> *Next: 'Never stop doubting... The humility required for good judgment is not self-doubt – the sense that you are untalented, unintelligent, or unworthy. It is intellectual humility. It is a recognition that reality is profoundly complex, that seeing things clearly is a constant struggle, when it can be done at all, and that human judgment must therefore be riddled with mistakes.' They cite the history of medicine and its barbarous quack remedies as an example of a centuries-long failure to put ideas to experimental test, because so few were willing to doubt that they were right. Their superforecasters talk in terms of probabilities, never black and white, and when they mention Zero Dark Thirty's story about knowing bin Laden was there, 100 per cent, it's not in a good way. For every confident forecaster who hits the mark, they can show you a confident forecaster who misses by miles next time – often the same forecaster.*

Almost my only quibble with *Superforecasting* – which I like a lot – is the title. It has swagger that Philip and Dan otherwise work hard to control. As they say, they're all for intellectual humility. In fact Philip, one of the most reflective, respectful voices I've come across, once joked that he wanted to call it *Surprisingly-Consistently-Above-Average-Forecasters*.

That's more like it. Even superforecasters make marginal gains on a limited set of questions, looking not far ahead. This is a big deal – forecasting is often a byword for bullshit and riding your luck – so any gain is big news. But 'super'? Not so sure about that. Surprisingly consistent and above average? Yep, I'll happily give them that and lead the applause. Though I get why the publisher wanted something brash and catchy.

But if there's overreach in the title, in other ways it's over-modest. Its value goes way beyond forecasting, to all decisions that include uncertainty – so, pretty much all deci-sions – and to all analyses of how the world is and how it works. Superforecasting ideas extend wherever we try to work out why things happen or will happen; they extend to all questions about causality: past, present, future. Bayesian thinking can serve them all, and superforcasters shine at trading-off different evidence to reach balanced, condi-tional, flexible and *uncertain* judgements about problems of all sorts.

Just so happens forecasting tournaments suggest their ideas tend to work. Uncertainty and flexible updating win, as they win for Annie Duke. My un-catchy title for this would be: *Surprisingly consistent validation through forecasting of some tricks for thinking better about a lot of other stuff too.*

Philip and Dan write:

In the popular mind, scientists generate facts and chisel them into granite tablets. This collection of facts is what we call 'science'. As the work of accumulating facts pro-ceeds, uncertainty is pushed back. The ultimate goal of science is uncertainty's total eradication. But that is a very nineteenth-century view of science. One of twentieth-century science's great accomplishments has been to show that uncertainty is an ineradicable element of reality... This is true both at the margin of scientific knowledge and at what currently appears to be its core. Scientific facts that look as solid as rock to one generation of scientists can be crushed to dust beneath the advances of the next. All scientific knowledge is tentative. Nothing is chiselled in granite.

They quote mathematician and statistician William Byers: 'Most people would identify science with certainty... Certainty, they feel, is a state of affairs with no downside, so the most desirable situation would be one of absolute certainty. Scientific results and theories seem to promise such certainty.' But they add: 'Uncertainty is real. It is the dream of total certainty that is an illusion.'

I'm an uncertainty evangelist – militantly at times. I see public argument as often a comedy of binaries, all sides running scared of uncertainty. This seems to me not just wrong, but bad strategy. There are advantages to an uncertain outlook on life, not least (as Annie says) it's more accurate, but also it gets you off the hook of repeated failure to know everything. So feel free to read this chapter as the rant of a fanatic, but while I have your attention, here's the rant...

There can be no progress between people who disagree – without uncertainty. Why talk at all, if you're both glued to 100 per cent? There can be no rethinking on our own without some chink of uncertainty to move through, so you'd better be 100 per cent right from the off or you're in trouble. Uncertainty means there's territory to explore. Uncertainty is the ground you must stand on if curiosity is to mean anything, if finding out is to mean anything, if there's to be any point to experiment. Without uncertainty, life would have no flavour of life. Can't live with uncertainty? OK, shall we tell you how all the films end? Want to know when and how you'll die? Want to know your Christmas presents for evermore, now? Want to know it all? Can't imagine anything more fatally, inhumanly dull.[10]

If you've not met before, time to introduce you to a dead aristocrat: Michel de Montaigne (1533–1592), now regarded as one of the great philosophers of the Renaissance, though to some people a simple essayist and – to both friend and critic alike – rambling, inconclusive and dripping with self-doubt. His catchphrase? *'Que sais-je?'* What do I know?

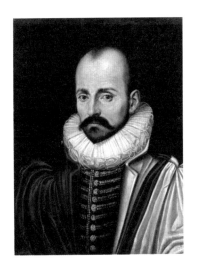

There are exactly two things that determine how our lives turn out: the quality of our decisions and luck. Learning to recognize the difference between the two is what thinking in bets is all about.

Annie Duke

**Michel de Montaigne,
history's most famous 'Erm...'**

There are no heroes in this book (never have heroes), so I thought twice about a portrait for our portrait gallery. But if anyone qualifies, it's Montaigne, who epitomised his ideas so entirely that he can stand for them. 'I am myself the matter of my book,' he wrote, finding even himself elusive: he wasn't sure what he thought about anything.

The French title of his work, *Essais*, or Attempts, announces its ignorance – all he can do is try, and fail, and try again, in eternal self-reappraisal. At times, Montaigne goes too far even for me, but to experience a truly uncertain mind – as he rethinks almost in real time, changes course mid-essay, puts one side, then another, doubts, then doubts his own doubts – there's nothing quite like reading Montaigne. It's not that he believes there's no truth. He just sees the fabulous ease of being confidently wrong: 'There is nothing certain but uncertainty,' he said, 'and nothing more miserable and arrogant than man.'

Not so fast

Another pile of caveats and objections.

1. Talking up uncertainty would be easy if only so many people didn't hate it, often paying for it with anxiety, and who'd want more of that? Can we be so *sure* other people's craving for certainty is so bad for them that we're entitled to try to destroy their confidence?

2. More trouble: there's tension between uncertainty and moral conviction. How far do we go in putting beliefs up for grabs? Must everything we believe be

uncertain? Conviction is often how we get things done. It can be motivating – and we need motivation. Did slavery's abolitionists spend time calibrating their uncertainty?

3. Are we sure uncertainty pays off? Funny if we were. It's easy to find counter-examples. Can anyone think of a politician, by any chance, who reached the heights while claiming to know it all? Maybe in the long-term truth catches up with them, but in the long-term, as John Maynard Keynes said, we're all dead.

4. We have a winning formula, says Philip Tetlock: lots of small updates. Except, he adds, what if we begin to suspect that a belief we've been changing slowly is more fundamentally out of whack? At that point, incremental change isn't enough. Each small piece of new evidence on its own might not make much difference, but cumulatively maybe they bring a tipping point. An example he gives is a superforecaster's doubts about the evidence for human-made climate change, a scepticism that bit-by-bit the superforecaster revised until he decided bit-by-bit wasn't enough. The weight of bits was beginning to look persuasive in a way that each bit didn't. He decided to reset. For a critical view of Bayesian updating, see *Realism for Realistic People* by Hasok Chang.

5. There's an insult thrown at leaders who see two sides to every problem: 'my indecision is final'. On the other hand, think Annie Duke didn't take decisions? She took

twenty every two-minute hand. It's false to say uncertainty prevents decisions, but it's true to say it can make them feel harder and it doesn't play to the gallery. Does that mean politics makes uncertainty naive?

Try this

Do we dislike uncertainty so much that we're wired to resolve it? It's sometimes said that the human brain is incapable of seeing two different perspectives at once. Try it visually with an example of the kind of famously ambiguous picture sometimes used to make the case that we're uncertainty- or ambiguity-averse. See if you can hold in mind both perspectives – the old woman and the young – in a state of uncertainty.

But what does it mean that it's hard to see both at once? Does it really mean the brain is uncertainty-averse? Experts disagree. Even the meaning of how we react to uncertain images is uncertain.

One for the gallery. Each perspective seems correct, until it changes. Is it neither? Is uncertainty the way? For me, yes. But as a reliable rule? Erm...

Another idea to try out: if there's an area you know well – say, you're a teacher – ask yourself how black-and-white the teaching gurus are. Do they insist that there is only one way, and their way is it? Is the science really that definitive?

The aim of science is not to open the door to infinite wisdom, but to set a limit to infinite error.

Bertolt Brecht

Old, young, both, neither?
My Wife and My Mother-In-Law
by cartoonist W. E. Hill.

Jargon

- *Integrative complexity*: the task akin to seeing both images at once – combining the perspectives of your dragonfly eyes.

Try this

Release your inner Bayesian on a story that's been running now for more than fifty years – the belief that knowledge of genetics will enable us to engineer people. Maybe you think it already has. Maybe you think we've had fifty years of hype. Maybe you haven't a clue – in which case points for recognizing your limitations. Try to calibrate your confidence in what can be achieved, and your doubt, given the history. Then put some probabilities on what'll be under the next card. If it helps, think of this as Annie Duke does – like belief calibration as new cards turn up. Note that there's no right answer, at least not yet.

1971

1981

1994

2011

2012

2015

2015

2016

?

Stick or twist. From an idea by Cecile Janssens.[11]

Trust in me. Front page of *The Sun*, 7 July 2014.

13

Don't trust

Seek trustworthiness

Confession time. A little of the right kind of smart-thinking can go a long way; I believe that, even if it's qualified by often being unsure which bit to use. But an even bigger qualifications is this: to assess claims properly in science, technology, psychology, economics, medicine, government, health, etc., all the smart-thinking in the world runs again and again into an old problem: to decide what we know or what's true, we must judge the quality of the finding-out.

That is, we're talking about the quality of the scientific or research method. We've put it off, aware it was coming. Well, here it is.

And here's the bad news. To understand method in the detail needed to tell good science or research from bad, to weigh the meaning and value of the original evidence... for that, smart-thinking often isn't nearly smart enough. Bad science can look frighteningly like good science, with all the trappings of rigour and smartness. To tell them apart, sometimes we need high-end expertise – very high-end – and the brutal truth is that much of this expertise is out of my league. If you're normal, it's out of yours.

When I started in this game, nothing was so alarming as the ease with which I was called an expert – nice, but not serious.

True expertise? I polish its boots. Many writers on smart-thinking are the same. Worse, proper expertise is beyond many scientists. No names, but there are eminent professors whose lunges into Covid-19 have been embarrassing. They decide they know better than the specialists (they don't), maybe neglect basic standards of research discipline or mock what the fools have missed (they haven't). Even I can spot when some have pushed off up the famed creek, paddle-less.

> To see how bad supposedly brainy stuff can be, and the skill needed to spot it, look up prediction models for the diagnosis and prognosis of Covid-19. These models sound complicated, but they are in principle trying to do something simple: to find out which symptoms or patient characteristics matter to the way things turn out – and therefore what to watch for, and who to worry about. These models often seem smart, they might use artificial intelligence, might be based on a mountain of data, might be published in high-quality journals.
>
> But as they poured out, a team of Dutch academics – serious specialists in prognostic modelling – began to evaluate these models. Here's my one-paragraph summary of their rolling review of the quality: there's a ton of these things, new ones come out all the time, ignoring the lessons of the others; almost all are dodgy, badly done, at high risk of bias, poorly reported and basically unreliable. Yet often the authors of these studies claim their models are fit for use on patients. It's been simultaneously intellectually flashy and a horror show. Smart people, not nearly smart enough, and not realizing it – like most of us.[1]

It's relatively easy to know, until it's not. Then it can be fiendish. Easy, too, to misjudge how hard it'll be – to think we're expert when we're still learning to tie our research shoelaces. There are plenty of experts who've said, 'We must trust the experts' (meaning them), when they've been winging it. And there are plenty of amateur sleuths whose investigations have led them down rabbit holes. To dig properly to the bottom of things, we might need both the people who know the subject inside out, plus others who know the whole caboodle of techniques for research methodology and interpreting the stats. A lot of this is deep, dark wonk territory, and I have huge respect for people who do it well. But back to the brutal truth, I can't. Not many can. So, what do we do?

A choice:

a) I could decide that, for all my limitations, I'm still good enough to be a research hero, maybe like the Hungarian scientist Ignaz Semmelweis, who took on the medical establishment over the causes of the slaughter in the nineteenth century that passed for maternity care in hospital (fatal infection in new mothers was rife). Semmelweis was a true pioneer of antiseptic medicine – almost alone and right (well, sort of) when the world was wrong.

Or would that be the most crashing act of self-delusion? After all, science has moved on since Semmelweis, and it's much harder now to find them all wrong, and to be right.

b) I could do what almost everyone does: ignore the motto of the Royal Society that we should never take other people's word for it – and take someone else's word for it.[2]

Let's say I'm lazy and decide not to be the kind of citizen scientist who revisits Isaac Newton's *Principia Mathematica* personally in search of errors,[3] and I choose B. I'll look to others for help.

Then there's a new problem. Which others? And why?

How about the people who say they're like Semmelweis – heroes taking on the consensus? People who know something others don't, they say. Or maybe like Barry Marshall and Robin Warren, who discovered that ulcers were caused by bacteria that had a simple cure, then had to fight for more than a decade to persuade the medical establishment?

Or should we take the word of the plodders who are part of the establishment consensus, who say listen to the consensus?

On the one hand, for every true Semmelweis there are a thousand wannabe Semmelweises who are just plain wrong. But once in a while it's the expert consensus that's wrong and there's a true Semmelweis who's right, or right enough. There *are* scandals; there *are* conspiracies; elites and experts do screw up; and there are lone pioneers who sometimes change the world.

For an extraordinary current example, look up the life and research of Katalin Karikó, the scientist behind synthetic messenger RNA, the basis of the Pfizer-BioNTech and Moderna vaccines against Covid-19, whose work was thought so hopeless that she couldn't get funding: 'Every night I was working: "grant, grant, grant". Every morning it came back "no, no, no,"' she once said. In the end, the vaccines were the work of thousands, but Katalin's part was often played alone, in the face of indifference.

> In the 1930s the right-thinking world thought Stalinist
> Russia a workers' utopia, a land of happiness and plenty.
> One journalist, Malcolm Muggeridge, escaped the usual
> control of Westerners and travelled by train to rural areas,
> where he saw terrible starvation. Stalin, we now know,

also ran a system of brutal internment camps, the gulags. Muggeridge tried to tell the Western media, smuggling out his reports in the diplomatic bag. He described skeletal people, whole towns shuffled away by secret police. No one believed him. Evidently he was some deranged fascist conspiracist. Western journalists who repeated the Russian line that all was sunlit uplands won prizes. Two academics in the West, Sidney and Beatrice Webb, wrote about the wonders of Stalinism and were revered. Between about five and eight million people are now thought to have died in the famine. If you'd trusted the experts, you'd have been fooled. If you'd listened to the mad dissenter, you'd have been right.

Today, some in the US allege that FEMA, a government agency for dealing with emergencies, is planning a system of internment camps for political dissenters. This time, if you listen to the experts that this is a mad conspiracy theory, you'll be right. Listen to the dissenters, you'll be fooled. But how do I know that for sure?

I owe this comparison to Scott Alexander, a leading voice in the world of rational thinking, who wrote:

> *...hearing all of these stories about the universal progressive Western adulation of Stalin is really* scary... *Part of my respect for contrarians is that contrarianism is this incredibly fragile and precious art which needs to be kept alive for the times it is needed – rare times, times that hopefully won't come up in our lifetimes, but times that, when they do come, desperately need a core of people willing to stand up to the establishment... Make absolutely sure*

> you're the sort of person who never misses a Stalinist
> gulag, and you become the type of person who's easy
> prey for the FEMA internment camp theory. Make
> absolutely sure you don't believe in FEMA internment
> camps, and you're liable to miss a Stalinist gulag as
> soon as [an expert says]: 'Oh, don't worry, that's only
> an Amtrak station'. Use the heuristic of 'just trust
> expert consensus, experts always know what they're
> talking about', and you are now one of the tens of
> thousands of grateful readers who helped make Sidney
> and Beatrice Webb's Soviet Communism: A New
> Civilisation into a best-seller.

Put our trust in the experts or the consensus and we miss a Semmelweis or a Muggeridge, or maybe a Barry Marshall and Robin Warren. Put our trust in a self-proclaimed Semmelweis and we risk sitting on a mountaintop wearing a tin-foil hat.

That's at the extremes of the problem, but it's no easier in the moderate range. There are a thousand shades of disagreement between even respected experts, and sometimes these disagreements are the fiercest. How do we amateurs judge? Who do we believe when they all speak the jargon and they all say 'me!'?

The temptation is to believe people we trust. Who do we trust? People who share our politics or values or prior beliefs: myside trust.

Bad idea. It's another route to confirmation bias.[4] My advice amid all the conflicting voices is to steer away from trust. Instead, adopt the principles of a still-groovy octogenarian philosopher, Baroness Onora O'Neill. What we want, Onora says, is not trust, but trustworthiness.[5]

What's the difference? Trustworthiness is not about who they are, their tribe or their answers; it's about how they show, by their actions, that they deserve to be trusted. Pay attention now, because this idea is going to do some heavy lifting.

Here's how I try to spot trustworthiness – my attempted synthesis of the books, of years of failing and learning and failing again, working with others like the Winton Centre[6] or BBC Radio 4's *More or Less* programme, and all the smarter people like Onora whose advice and practice I've lovingly ripped off. But note that nothing works perfectly. Their ideas can be used to help us try to get the measure of scientific evidence, but also the measure of almost anyone making a claim about how it is.

1. I start with the extreme end of the problem by doubting the outsider hero. Common in movies, vanishingly rare in life. I set a high probability against the rightness of anyone with the air of wannabe superhero. Not impossible, just highly unlikely. And their behaviour has a lot to do with that judgement. If they relish their outsider status – if they enjoy self-promotion, or they're 'mavericks' – I start to wonder what they're in it for. The very few who come close to credibility (there are some) need a pedigree in good method longer than your arm before I find them remotely trustworthy. If they tell you they're fighting evil, my scepticism bar is near the ceiling.

    Problem is, that's not far off a description of Semmelweis and Muggeridge. Semmelweis accused hospitals of mass murder; Muggeridge alleged mass starvation. Muggeridge was right, Semmelweis near enough. Other dissenters even today are similarly both angry and right. Even so, I'll stick with the anti-superhero stance simply as a probabilistic 99:1-against starting point. I once heard it put like this: scientific elites often get things wrong; anti-scientific elites usually get them far wronger. Because although it's true the mainstream can't always be trusted, it's crazy to assume therefore that the maverick wannabe super-hero can be.

So I make my bet, and it's almost always against the kind of people who really want you to know that they know it all and the rest are fools. Semmelweis and Muggeridge spent much of their lives disgusted with themselves and their failures – they did not feel like heroes, though it's also true they didn't think much of anyone else, either. Katalin Karikó – who did all that work on mRNA and was not a maverick, but was often a lonely voice – worked patiently, quietly, inside the system, mostly on a university payroll. She did not act the hero; she did her research. The more someone plays the saviour, or won't countenance disagreement, or treats questions with disdain while projecting a fluent, know-all self-assurance, the more guru-like, the less I like it. That kind of confidence is untrustworthy – whoever it comes from. And that's my first heuristic.

In 2022 a group of unpaid, self-appointed data police exposed the tat that passed at that time for the scientific study of Ivermectin – an anti-parasite drug – to treat Covid-19. Maybe one day we'll find Ivermectin could work against Covid in some small way, but I doubt it. Early studies endorsing it were bad, some likely fraudulent. But it took this ragbag of vigilantes to notice, do the hard analysis and accord this 'research' the lack of respect it deserved. Why did I believe these outsiders?

A few quick reasons. One, they're experts in method, they demonstrably swim in the deep end and, what mattered here (as we've said before) was the quality of the finding out – that word we had back near the beginning: 'reliability'.

Two, their lack of skin in the Covid game was also reassuring. They weren't selling rival pills, or jabs, or anything Covid-related, and they weren't paid for their research.

Three, I know a bit about their track record and a lot of their identity is invested in good method. If I gave them a study to check, I'd have no idea how they'd call it on any subject; they'd expose bad research that warns about climate change, they'd expose bad climate scepticism, they'll set research credibility above the answer they might like personally, every time. So, for this kind of job, they seem trustworthy.

Four, I think I know just enough method to understand what they're on about, and they sound legit to me – for example, that the size of the claimed benefit from Ivermectin in some of these studies was improbably ginormous.

Five, there's a stack of poor research out there on Covid-19, so I'm not surprised they found some, especially where the politics were excitable.

Six, they don't think they're saving the world. On the whole, they come across weary and despairing that the

> *job of exposing outrageously bad published research needs to be done at all.*
>
> *Even so, this a judgement. Next stage? To watch for bigger, better studies of Ivermectin, then update my judgement. When these began to come in, they strongly backed the self-appointed data police.*

2. If there's any easy progress that I can make on my own by checking methods, assumptions, data sources, etc., I will, but I'll try to watch my limitations.

   After that, it gets murky. I've reached my limits, and there are no strong clues like a pretender with a Messiah complex to steer away from. We're now in the mainstream. But still there are big disagreements between acknowledged experts. Worse, even some of the self-appointed arbiters of quality are unreliable, some of the rules they preach for reliability are dodgy. So we can't be guided by those who simply proclaim a commitment to truth and accuracy. What gets into a journal isn't a guarantee of rigour, either.[7]

   This is the riskiest part of the neighbourhood. It could all be plausible, it could all be wrong; some could be junk, and a lot has been. So back again to the problem: who do I trust around here? How do I differentiate between conflicting views within what passes for the mainstream?

3. Mainly, I look for the trustworthy. That is, I trust people not for their views necessarily, but for their behaviour and research values. For example, I respect more those who respect uncertainty.[8] For me, this

is a big test of people's claim to be taken seriously. I'm reassured when someone's speech/paper/article shows honest, prominent interest in the quality of evidence, its limitations and uncertainties, not just a token last paragraph. This suggests an interest in finding out how it is, not in selling their favourite conclusion. When I see honest respect for uncertainty, I see people like Annie Duke and Philip Tetlock's superforecasters, people with a deep commitment to good calibration of what we know. Experts who stray off their own turf to put the world to rights are prime candidates for this test.

'Oh yeah?' you say. Then what about the rogues who exploit uncertainty for their own dodgy ends – to sell more fags, for example, knowing there was little real uncertainty about their health effects, but playing it up anyway – as the foulest of these merchants of doubt tried to do, by grabbing every hint of uncertainty in the link between smoking and cancer? Can't uncertainty be a sign of the *un*trustworthy?

That's fair, and it's true these types are a menace. The kind of uncertainty we're looking for is good-faith uncertainty, and there's no sure way to tell good faith from bad. But there are clues. Respecting uncertainty means *not* attacking or exploiting it, or claiming it invalidates everything, and it means not apologizing for it, either. Respecting it also means stating it clearly and – here's the key – stating it on *all* sides of a question; i.e. the more uncertainty about the extent of climate change, the more chance the climate could turn out better – *or worse* – than expected, both. If you argue it's uncertain and so 'meh...', your uncertainty is loaded. Don't be nervous of uncertainty, don't shy from it, insist on it: from everyone. Ever noticed how often the mavericks question their own stuff? Or the conspiracists? Almost never, is my experience. Real science is willing to challenge itself; pseudo-science isn't. Climate sceptics love doubt, sure, but about their own position? Those willing to state uncertainties in their own position, and not just attack other people's, look to me more like trustworthy people. That's one of my biggest rules of thumb.

4. Similarly, ask yourself if their rigour is selective, or the evidence strangely all on one side. Looking at how people treat the full balance of evidence – for and against their own position – is my next big test. What's the totality of the evidence (even if only in summary)?

   If you have a chance, aim a question at your sources, as suggested by Andrew Gelman, a statistician I like: 'Who can you connect me to who would be sceptical of your finding?... Not someone they don't like, or don't trust, but someone they trust who disagrees. Anyone who is a real scientist would know such a person.'

5. Next another question: is what this dude tells me designed to inform, or is it to persuade? It's not much asked, but I like it. 'Inform' is like the weather forecast, telling us how it is, best they can, full of maybes, no real skin in the game. 'Persuade'? Anywhere from a

reasoned argument to selling a used car when they need us to be impressed, and we know why.

In case anyone's struggling, here's the dictionary:

- *Inform*: give facts or information.
- *Persuade*: induce someone to do or believe something through reason, evidence or argument.

The distinction's far from perfect. Pure, balanced information without a hint of persuasion is hard to do. Even the order in which evidence is presented can tilt the scales. In practice, most of what we're told includes both. And one's not right and the other wrong. If the theatre's on fire, persuasion to get out fast can be fair enough.

Imperfect then, but still useful, and the reason is that according to where a message sits on the line from inform to persuade, so my belief shifts. Crudely, the more persuasion from them, the more scepticism from me. That's born of the belief – is this naive? – that good information, fairly interpreted, shouldn't need a hard sell, and anyone who tries is maybe so invested in the answer that they may be less rigorous.

Doesn't mean that I accept or reject their evidence there and then. But the second I feel they're sexing it up, the more I mark them down. The more leaned on, the more I lean back. Hype makes me twitchy. If persuasion claims to be 'just giving you the facts', but it's evidently more than that, it's blown any goodwill and now has a hill to climb. If, on the other hand, it seems to be genuinely trying to tell it like it is, without its thumbs in the scale, that alone is mildly reassuring. Not conclusive, but it wins points. I feel capable of sounding the alarm if the evidence – fairly presented – is alarming. But in general, if you want to appear trustworthy, keep your boots off my lawn.

So, inform is not truth, and persuade is not lies, but it's an early steer on trustworthiness.

Don't know about the war in Iraq. Think it was probably an avoidable disaster that also wrecked the West's moral authority. But given what was known, there's room for doubt. Tony Blair, then British prime minster, famously said he had none, and gave war a hard sell. Iraq already had, or was hell-bent on, weapons of mass destruction (WMD), he said, and it was ridiculous to think otherwise (wrong, we learned later). So maybe this was one man who called a war how he saw it, and for that should have been trusted. But was his behaviour trustworthy?

In the run-up to the war, the British government asked its Joint Intelligence Committee to assess the threat from WMD. A subsequent inquiry said: 'The Government wanted a document on which it could draw in its advocacy of its policy. The JIC sought to offer a dispassionate assessment' (my emphasis). What landed was a mixture, as wording was reportedly 'strengthened'. 'Sexed up', the media called it. Whatever, the intention was to make it more persuasive. It became known as 'the dodgy dossier'.

If you believe this account, the JIC tried to be more like a weather forecaster, but the government was selling. Some didn't care. They believed in war anyway.

I think if the case was there, it didn't need sexing up, but suspect they were terrified of acknowledging the extent of the uncertainty about those WMD (their intelligence sources weren't exactly twenty-four-carat reliable, but they weren't about to say so). By suppressing the uncertainty – consciously or not – the government hoped to be more persuasive. Instead, it positively invited mistrust.

Sorry, Tony, but I'm going to make you the poster boy for the difference between seeking trust and being trustworthy. You say your sincere belief is what matters. I think your methods are a better measure. If it's any comfort, I find a lot of politicians the same: they want trust, they daren't do trustworthy. 'Uncertainty, are you kidding? I'd be ripped apart.' They should read Chapter 12.

I Can't Believe What You Say (For Seeing What You Do)

Tina Turner
(song of that name)

Motives are messy. They're in it for money, in someone's pocket, is one suspicion, if often a lazy one. Because maybe they are, but maybe there's also pride, the public good, ambition, conscience, duty, fear, love, vanity, obligation, guilt, reputation, power – you name it – in any combination. Sometimes we see these motives clearly for what they are. Often they're too messy to put down to one impulse. By comparison, spotting persuasion is a simple if inconclusive test that's a little easier to apply.

Now, scientific papers... The convention is they simply convey the results of experiments or research, that's it. But as Gareth and Rhodri Ivor Leng say in The Matter of Facts: *'In reality, all scientists are in the business of persuading other scientists of the importance of their own ideas, and they do so by combining reason with rhetoric. Often, they look for evidence that will support their ideas, not for evidence that might contradict them; often, they present evidence in a way that makes it appear to be supportive; and often, they ignore inconvenient evidence.'*

By keeping inform-persuade in mind, it becomes a little easier to see if their PR is getting the better of them. Those rhetorical tricks can sometimes be spotted, even when we're not expert enough to weigh up the evidence itself. Hints they're edging further into persuasion territory include the 'simple take-home message', the 'call to action', reliance on storytelling, a whole heap of evidence on a controversial question but all strangely on one side (if you're not seeing balanced evidence, you're not seeing evidence, you're seeing advertising), sliding from a weak association to claims of causation. Try to become attuned to small (and large) acts of sexing up.

Partly, the worry is that those most keen to persuade us, or their publishers, or politicians, or prospective employers, might be equally keen to persuade themselves, because they know the answer they want.

Too many scientific papers fail to replicate, too many contain what are known as questionable research practices (QRPs). While in one way failure is fine – it happens – you have to wonder how much of this failure is due to good ol' motivated reasoning and a desire to persuade.

6. Do they discuss the quality of their evidence? A claim that eighteen oranges a day cured my dad's dementia is huge – but the quality could be useless. Research that seems to try honestly to evaluate the quality of its own evidence gets marks; research that just says 'this changes everything' loses them.

7. Trustworthiness is bounded. I trust my dentist with my teeth, not for research on Covid-19. I want at least some evidence of relevant competence. Being a physics professor jumping into Covid is not of itself impressive, much as diverse perspectives can *sometimes* be useful. Those research vigilantes I mentioned? I trust them on research method. On taste in music, there's one I wouldn't trust with a toothbrush.

8. A few other marks of trustworthiness, or not... Does new evidence seem always to confirm whatever

they've always said? If so, are they assessing that
evidence or bullying it? Are they frank about mistakes
or do they absurdly never make any, or blame them
all on others? Do they make their data freely available,
where possible? Is their evidence in a form I can use?
Do they tell me their sources? Broadly, do they show
me their workings and commit to good method and
talk about it? Do they seem willing to trust me with
information or do they filter for 'the right message'?
Do they seem eager to advocate big policy change
on the tails of their research, do they go on about its
massive implications? Do they claim to know about a
small area or a large one?

Those are a few of the things I watch for. Not exhaustive, and
highly fallible, but useful for forming a surface impression of
trustworthiness. By comparison, here are a few other, let's say,
insufficient clues of trustworthiness that we might find tempting:

They're Republican/Democrat/Labour/Conservative/Lib Dem/
SNP/Green, etc./outsiders/radical/established/in authority/
in business/in academia/work for a charity/think-tank/govern-
ment/use data/are psychologists/economists/'scientists'/
historians/appear full of conviction/certain/consistent/have a
big job/are rich/have published in a science journal/are good-
looking/fluent/outspoken or controversial/new, fresh, original,
'brave' or 'daring' or dramatic... [9]

These are what get people on TV or retweeted; these are
the labels we notice and maybe trust, depending on where we
stand. Sod trust. Look for trustworthiness.

Smart-thinking can sometimes show us a killer route to the
truth. More likely, the truth is complicated and uncertain and

we rely heavily on others. To go as far as we can, we might need very high-level expertise; and sometimes even that makes howling mistakes. I said at the start that smart-thinking began with seeing through ourselves; and we could deal with other people's stupidity later. Well, it's later. But now we're here and wondering how to see through competing experts, smart-thinking turns out to be out of its depth, not equipped to assess what they say. But what it can do – where it's still useful – is help us judge how they say it.

That is, smart-thinking's last line of defence is to help spot the players who aren't trying to follow basic smart-thinking advice, such as: respect uncertainty, try to weigh evidence fairly, highlight the weakness in your own arguments, challenge your own assumptions, and so on; basically, those who don't walk the walk. If smart-thinking behaviours are right for us, they're right for them. This might not tell us who's definitely right, but it can sometimes clear out a dodgy voice or two. If they don't have these marks of trustworthiness, I don't care how hard they're selling, or even what – I'll buy elsewhere.

Not so fast

1. Beware: trustworthiness can be gamed. Well, up to a point. People can pretend to be helpful, pretend to be open, reflective, even-handed, to respect uncertainty, all the while cheating like crazy. And though we often see through them in the end, that end is a long way off. Until it arrives, layers of deceit can make it hard to be sure what we're looking at.

2. Meanwhile, honest, reasonable people can fall foul of a rule against persuasion. Their urge to sell can be innocent, even good. 'What I've discovered is so critical and alarming, the world must act now!' Should we doubt them for that? Not always. Persuasion has its place. But is the best place in research or in politics? In politics, persuasion is unavoidable. Almost everything a government wants to do takes votes, or you don't get the power to do it. That means campaigning and persuasion.

But alongside that, we need to uphold a value-free ideal *somewhere*, however hard. Science and research are often said to be that somewhere, and it's easy to see why. This helps sustain trustworthiness in a democracy. If we suspect that researchers don't even set out to treat the evidence neutrally, hard as that is, why trust their evidence or their method? If they don't think they have any obligation even to try to be neutral, I wonder what they think we're paying them for. Is that pious or naive? On this one, I'm willing to be both.[10]

3. Even when you've decided only to trust the trustworthy, you might still have more than one person with more than one answer about what's true, so then what do you do? Which is another way of saying that even the trustworthy can be wrong. There are no guarantees here. All you can do is place your bets, with all the risks that entails.

4. Finally... No matter how full of caveats, counterarguments and 'not-so-fasts', this book also tries to

persuade, if only to persuade you that smart-thinking is trickier than it looks. Should you disbelieve this book because it, too, has a persuasive streak? Is the whole thing a piece of hypocrisy?

All smart-thinking books try to persuade. Do you feel leaned on? Do authors' interests in selling books mean they inflate the value of their ideas? You don't know their true motives, but you might recognize persuasion when you see it. Clock that fact. How much does it shape the content? Adjust your reactions accordingly, stay curious and sceptical – of me included.

Try this

Get bolshie. People who want to persuade often use selective information, cherry-picked data or other tricks to steer our attention. 'Framing', it's sometimes called. So now and then, just to explore the evidence, it can pay to be contrary and refuse to be framed the way they want.

First, work out where you're expected to look, then look elsewhere. We'll reserve the right to decide what evidence is relevant, thanks all the same. We'll decide if we're happy with where you're pointing us, what to count, etc. For example...

Climate change is real, caused by us, serious. That said, here goes. The Guardian reported that climate change would drive up the number of people who died from summer heat. True, according to the research it quoted. But even within its own narrow terms – deaths from temperature change – this puts only one part of the evidence in the frame. What's excluded from this story about death from rising heat (that's a clue)?

Answer: cold. How many would normally die of cold during winter, but would survive if temperatures rose? That is, climate change might also save some lives. But why would we think to ask about cold or saving lives, when the story's about death from heat? Maybe if we're bolshie.

This story reported one side of the balance sheet, the potential lives lost to heat, but ignored potential lives saved from cold. It didn't lie, but if you think that's enough, you're in the wrong book. The overall balance – at least according to the Guardian's source, not reported by the Guardian itself – was that more would be saved in winter than killed in summer. That's what I mean by being bolshie: if they say hot, you ask cold. If they look at lives lost, you ask about lives saved. (NB: this is in the UK, and according to this research it's not true elsewhere, and it's only one part of the overall effect of climate change.)

Similarly, if they say here, in cities, you think about there, in the country. They say old, you ask about young. They say it's all about a fight between old and young, you ask if it isn't about poor and rich that cuts across both. They talk about what happened in the last five years, you ask about the last ten. If they talk about the data for success, start wondering about

> *the data for failure. They want to think of it mathe-matically, you ask about it socially, ethically or maybe emotionally, and so on. They hit you with large-scale data, you look for personal stories. They give you per-sonal stories, you look for data. They say theory, you say pragmatism. After a while, it becomes a reflex. It might not tell you anything new, but* Vive la résistance!

We can't always be like Gillian Tett and see what everyone else missed, but we can all practise little acts of contrariness against being steered or framed. There's value in this bolshiness and it's different from being a naysayer or trying to change the subject; it's to insist on your right to try to be a dragonfly.

Jargon

- *Accessible, useable, assessable*: not quite jargon, but Onora O'Neill's three rules for what trustworthy evidence should be. Can you get at the evidence and data, so you're not relying only on the conclusion? Do you have enough clear information to assess its quality and robustness? And is it in a form that enables you to make practical use of it? If it doesn't tick these boxes, can you trust it?

*Beliefs are hypotheses to be
tested, not treasures to be guarded.*

Philip Tetlock and Dan Gardner

14

Get a new attitude

Work your curiosity

Two mindsets described by Julia Galef in *The Scout Mindset*:

1. The soldier: defensive, aggressive, maybe both, but basically out to kick ass, the soldier is hyper-territorial. Thinking is a fight, evidence an ally or a threat. You have a side. You win or lose.

2. The scout: curious and exploratory, the scout sets out to survey the territory, not to defend or conquer, and above all to bring back an accurate map. Julia defines this mindset as: 'the motivation to see things as they are, not as you wish they were'. Thinking is discovery.

Guess which she recommends? (Btw, I think she meant an army scout more than a Boy Scout. But for a picture, I've gone for the sunniest kind.[1])

Among published smart-thinkers that I read, none says the goal should be to kick ass (there are other genres for that). True to type, Julia wants us to work on a positive-vibe smart-thinking, where nothing matters like the truth and honest curiosity is the way, and the only things you kick are the tyres.

She makes a good case, on two grounds:

1. For the sake of your well-being (less stress from feeling you're in a war zone).

2. Results (whatever you want to achieve, knowing the truth beats being deceived). The curious and truth-driven see things clearly when others don't.

What sets this argument apart is the claim that smart-thinking doesn't work if you treat it as a set of tech skills to solve tech problems. That's not what makes the difference here. As the science replication saga suggested, tech skills are easily abused. Early on Julia repeats a line that you hear from other smart-thinking early adopters: 'I finally came to accept that *knowing how to reason* wasn't the cure-all I thought it was.'

But if knowing how to reason – and knowing the rules, principles and ideas of smart-thinking – doesn't do it, then what does?

For Julia, the absolute must-have, bottom line, without which everything else is unreliable, is... (drum roll): attitude. You must *want* to see things as they are. In this sense, good reasoning requires motivation after all, but it's the motivation to seek the truth, irrespective of whose side it's on.

For Tim Harford too, it's an attitude – curiosity – which is the golden rule that he says informs every other, in his book *How to Make the World Add Up.* Curiosity and Julia's scout-mindset are peas in a pod. Both really want to know what's up, no sneaky stuff, no confirmation bias, no cheating, as pure and simple as we can discover it. And the good news is that we all have curiosity in us. It also makes us less tribal, helps to generate good evidence and it can be cultivated. What's not to like (though, curiously, curiosity hasn't always been thought a virtue[2])?

A seductive argument, and I'm seduced, mostly. But before we move on in the belief that a shiny new attitude will see us smarter and smiling, a few obstacles, beginning with words you also occasionally find in smart-thinking – but probably not enough – with a different vibe.

1. **Pain**: thinking, said John Dewey in 1910, is 'a state of perplexity, hesitation, doubt'. Sounds no fun at all, and there's more: 'Reflective thinking is always more or less troublesome because it involves... willingness to endure a condition of mental unrest and disturbance. Reflective thinking, in short, means judgement suspended during further inquiry; and suspense is likely to be somewhat painful. To maintain the state of doubt and to carry on systematic and protracted inquiry – these are the essentials of thinking.'

   If it's not hurting, are you doing it right?

2. **Failure**: we're all wrong from time to time. We go nowhere if we can't say so and learn from it. Pride or ego can be one of the great barriers to accepting error or failure (see confirmation bias, myside bias, self-justification, etc.). If you're such a snowflake that you need to be right all the time, you tell yourself a lot of lies. So reasoning better often means prising yourself from the grip of ego and accepting more failure. If you read smart-thinking to be successful, this could be hard going.

3. **Stupidity**: 'If you're not feeling stupid it means you're not really trying,' says Martin Scharwtz, a microbiologist.[3] This is elective stupidity, when you pick your stupidity carefully: 'Productive stupidity means being ignorant by choice,' he says, by recognizing where we need to learn. Might not feel good, but it's a lot better than being unproductively stupid, or than simply reinforcing what you think you already know.

4. **Frustration**: in the same spirit as **3**. Stuff is *hard*, said Brian Christian and Tom Griffiths in *Algorithms to Live By*, so if your answers come easily, maybe you're missing something. Expect empiricism to take time, expect experiments to go wrong for unseen reasons, expect a lot of tweaking, expect painful rebukes from life's afterthoughts.

5. **Boredom**: there's a problem, says Carl Bergstrom, whose book on smart-thinking is called *Calling Bullshit*; research that tests your new miracle idea and finds that actually nothing much happens is so disappointing that no one wants to know or, as he puts it: '*I tried x but it didn't work* is boring.' From here, a host of bad thinking follows. Because these null results are dull, we filter them out or just don't talk about them. Who cares about a non-discovery? That biases our whole perception of the state of knowledge. If we focus only on the new, trending or exciting, and ignore the ordinary, pedestrian or disappointing, we're seeing only half the evidence, and nothing like a balanced half. But note: truth is indifferent to excitement. To think well, and hear balanced evidence, be willing to be bored.

6. **Abuse**: you also have the problem of what other people say and think about you, and they might be brutal when you start sharing your errors, failures, uncertainties, second thoughts, etc. So expect abuse. That's not easy to bear – not if you were banking on strutting your smartness. Fear of criticism can make conformists of us all, maybe enforcers of conformity. All this constrains thinking. To resist, we need either bravery or resilience, or maybe indifference (I am not brave). What'll you do, scout, it they shoot at you?

Some of this is a technical pain; it takes work and patience to overcome. Most of it is emotional pain – it just feels bad. Reassure me: you didn't buy this book to feel good, did you? Or because you thought pictures could tell you what to think? You weren't looking for answers?

Good. Because we're not gathered to solve problems. We're here to cause them. Answers aren't thinking. Answers are to thinking like the last frame to the whole movie. My guess is that some readers of smart-thinking are looking for ways to cut to that frame where everything is sorted. They'd like to be spared discomfort or change. 'The rage to conclude' Edward Tufte called this. Some books want to sell exactly that appearance of quick wins. Too bad. You first have to do the work, and that means being willing positively to seek out discomfort.

One book that's clear that thinking can be tough on the thinker is *How to Think* by Tom Chatfield. Short, no rhetorical fireworks, no magic bullets; just careful, wise and realistic about what it takes. Tom says early on, 'Serious thinking is an effortful, even a painful business... it always entails some conflict between the desire for certainty (and thus for clarity

An armchair for armchair experts. If it doesn't feel like this, maybe you're doing something wrong. Remember this 'chair' from earlier? Do sit down. Make yourself uncomfortable.

when it comes to actions and beliefs) and the systematic sus-
pension of judgement associated with intellectual inquiry.'

> *How's this for wretched: a feeling so bad, some smart-
> thinkers say, it's almost never acknowledged, and we'll
> think and do almost anything to avoid it? This feeling is
> cognitive dissonance, first named by the social psycholo-
> gist Leon Festinger. It's what happens when you want to
> believe in people or their decisions, or maybe in yourself –
> your judgement, wisdom and behaviour – but then along
> comes awkward counter-evidence to suggest you were a
> muttonhead. What do you do?*
>
> *Usually, fight it. In* Mistakes Were Made (but Not by
> Me)*, Carol Tavris and Elliot Aronson say that rather than
> endure cognitive dissonance, we'll find ways to justify the
> most foolish beliefs and decisions, we'll double-down,
> we'll imagine reasons that never were, blame someone
> else, and so on. They cite criminals and tyrants as those
> who somehow find a way to justify dire or stupid behav-
> iour; but also, more arrestingly, themselves. All of us
> self-justify to escape the dissonant feeling that maybe
> we weren't as wise or good as we'd like to think we
> were. 'How do you get an honest man to lose his ethical
> compass?' they ask. 'You get him to take one step at a
> time, and self-justification will do the rest.' So if you want
> to see* all *the evidence and use those dragonfly eyes, first
> come to terms with cognitive dissonance.*
>
> *But there's one more twist to this celebrated piece of
> smart-thinking: some of Leo Festinger's research results
> on cognitive dissonance were found a few years ago to
> contain data that was internally inconsistent, meaning*

> *some of it couldn't be true. That doesn't necessarily destroy the theory, but if you're attracted to it, it sure is awkward; maybe even cognitively dissonant.*[4]

'How does it feel?' Tim Harford says we should ask, when we take in evidence or information. It's a terrific question, nagging us to reflect on our hopes, anxieties and expectations, to alert ourselves to whatever makes us resistant or keen – everything that tempts us to see evidence partially (and a clue about how people might be trying to manipulate our feelings). If it feels good, or bad, is that feeling already making us biased? Is it a sign we're being played?

That question invites another: if we want to see evidence clearly, should we try to set feelings aside or even confront them, interrogate them, because of the risk they could be in the way of truth?

And if you say 'yes', then how far should that confrontation go? Feelings can run deep. They're often expressions of our whole identity. Must we chase them all the way down? What would that mean?

The social psychologist Jonathan Haidt has a vivid metaphor for what challenging our feelings entails, so let's have a picture. He asks us to imagine a rider on an elephant, clueless how to control it: 'The rider is our conscious reasoning,' he says in *The Righteous Mind*, 'the stream of words and images of which we are fully aware. The elephant is the other 99 per cent of mental processes – the ones that occur outside of awareness but that actually govern most of our behaviour.'

What are these dominant mental processes of which we're unaware? Emotion and intuition, which, he says, are automatic, the thoughts or feelings that say, 'That's just wrong!'

Who's in charge here?

These feelings about what's right and wrong are shaped by all kinds of forces: the culture that tells us eating dogs is 'just wrong', for example, or a personal experience buried in our past. Once adopted, these feelings quickly become righteous and tribal, he says. If other people don't conform, they're not just wrong, they're bad. Try this out on any number of your feelings about big social questions involving fairness, rights or freedoms, asking yourself how you feel about people who disagree.

As the rider of the elephant, you think conscious reason steered you to your conclusions, but often reason is simply along for the ride, Jonathan says, 'skilled at fabricating post hoc explanations for whatever the elephant has just done... good at finding reasons to justify what the elephant wants to do next'.

So when asking 'how does it feel?', it could be that we're taking on the elephant, the huge 99 per cent of all mental pro-cesses that are more like feeling than reason. 'If you want to change people's minds, you've got to talk to their elephants,' he says. Which means, I guess, that if you want conscious self-direction, you need a serious talk with your own elephant. Check the picture, imagine the conversation.

The way I'm inviting you to think about this is that 'How does it feel?' is a great question, but if Jonathan's right, it means judging yourself all the way down, and it might require a kind of colossal self-mutiny. We're not well equipped for this, he argues. Just 1 per cent of what drives us – the 1 per cent that's conscious reasoning – is all the resource we have to master the elephant, when it was originally designed to serve the elephant. This unequal struggle adds to all the pain and other aggro we've talked about. Is that what 'How does it feel?' implies? If you buy Jonathan's analogy, it seems unavoidable.

There was once a view that this separation of conscious

reasoning and feeling, to allow one to challenge the other, was impossible. You can't split yourself in two, the argument went. That view has recently been revived, and has thought and feeling wholly co-dependent.[5] Jonathan Haidt, a leading voice in the emotions faction of smart-thinking, goes so far as to say that the worship of reason is 'an example of faith in something that does not exist' – the elephant already dominates the consciousness that would challenge it. If he's right, that's one heck of an obstacle.

There's another. Sometimes, a scout's commitment to truth will cost the scout dear, literally. Science itself can be in this category, as the dodgy research practices discovered in recent years (whether conscious or not) can profit an individual career – and often have. Hype can get you published. In a perverse way, you might even say bad research can be rational if it helps you get on. Prizes, jobs, recognition have gone to people with questionable attitudes to go with their questionable research practices, and some of them don't seem to mind their soldiering one bit. Clearly this can be actively bad for the truth, so scouting would have to renounce it.

All told, scouting begins to sound less smiley and more bruising.

Let's gather our metaphors for a little homily: the temple of honest curiosity is reached by the chair of pain and taming the elephant of feeling. Are you up for that, Scout?

And so, having made ourselves uncomfortable, having confronted ourselves over who we are and how we feel, and having realized that any change might hurt... to the crunch: can Julia's attitude-shift make all this OK: the pain, uncertainty, boredom, failure, mockery, dissonance, potential personal cost and the challenge to our own deep feelings?

That is, can attitude and love of curiosity: a) help bring about a transfer of power away from the elephant in favour of effective conscious reasoning and a commitment to truth; and b) make it feel, if not exactly a frolic in the park, then maybe less like pulling teeth?

If Jonathan's right that people are in some ways ill-designed for this, maybe there's also a c) – can a new attitude work better for us than the evolution that built us? One reviewer suggested the soldier mindset should simply be called the human mindset, making the scout mindset what? The inhuman mindset?

I wouldn't go that far. As I say, I'm on Julia and Tim's side here. But at the very least there's a strong 'eat your greens' feel to the scout/curiosity case. It'll do us good, genuinely make us smarter and it will feel better in the end, honestly it will. In the future you will be grateful; you'll grow to like broccoli.

The reason I'm still onside is that whatever our evolved tastebuds tell us, whatever our feelings and cravings, somehow many people do eat their greens and do grow to like them, and tend to be healthier. And you've also noticed that people *are* curious. That's in us too, not just the ego-stroking, tribal delusions; and quite likely curiosity also evolved because it proved useful. It can feel good. And it does often pay off. Likewise, many scientists do have an ethic that trumps narrow self-interest.[6] And although no technique is fail-safe, somehow, despite it all, we do seem capable – erratically, messily, but capable – of advancing our understanding.[7] Plus, you have to ask: if not this, then what?

Julia – wise to the obstacles – says: 'Yes, we often rationalize away our mistakes – but sometimes we acknowledge them, too. We change our minds less often than we should, but more often than we could. We're complex creatures who sometimes hide the truth from ourselves and sometimes confront it.'

At the children's home where my son Joe first went when we finally accepted we couldn't look after him any more – he has profound developmental and behavioural difficulties – there was another boy with a condition that meant his sleep–waking cycle was absurdly long. He could do both for days. His care involved trying to regularize his hours, waking him and keeping him going when he was desperate for sleep. The carers told me it had to be this way, but it looked merciless. They'd have him on the trampoline, trying to get him going, while he longed to curl up and close his eyes. At best, smart-thinking, curiosity, discovery, even uncertainty can be a blast, or as natural as breathing. At worst, I think of that boy on the trampoline, trying to keep his eyes open, longing for sleep.

But you made it this far. Maybe you're a natural. If so, you won't be banking on it.

Try this

1. Pick a subject you care about, maybe feel strongly about. Then set out to cause yourself as much cognitive dissonance as you can by challenging it as if it were evil on Earth. See how long you can keep it up. Reflect on what it does to you.

2. Keep your identity small, said the writer and investor Paul Graham in a short, influential essay: 'People can never have a fruitful argument about something

that's part of their identity. By definition they're partisan...'[8]

'Most people reading this will already be fairly tolerant,' he wrote. 'But there is a step beyond thinking of yourself as x but tolerating y: not even to consider yourself an x. The more labels you have for yourself, the dumber they make you.' What's intriguing about this theory, he said, is that it would explain how to have better ideas: 'If people can't think clearly about anything that has become part of their identity, then all other things being equal, the best plan is to let as few things into your identity as possible.'

Not easy, and for people who feel their identity faces hostility, this will be more of the same: more repression, more demands for self-censorship so as not to offend. They might answer, 'Better ideas don't come from repressing my identity, they come from accepting and celebrating it. That's when we get somewhere.' So it's the usual again, I'm afraid: not too fast with the anti-identities. Not too fast, either, with asserting them.

15

Last thoughts

The ideas in smart-thinking are great (mostly), the writers classy and clever (as they should be), but the doubts — some we've touched on — are more extensive than you might expect. Such as:

1. Whether ordinary mortals are up to practising what's preached, and if what's preached is too narrow and inhuman a definition of smart or rational, being often concocted in the lab as if people should be infinite calculating machines.

2. Whether some smart-thinking ends up self-serving, smug and culturally specific — that is, biased!

3. Whether too much treats reasoning like a private calculation, a tool to enhance your competitive edge (basically selfish), when really we should be more focused on the social and political arguments that no amount of private calculation can fix on its own.

4. Whether the technical fixes even work as advertised, partly because it isn't clear when to apply them because you don't know what the problem is.

5. Teaching general cognitive skills is probably pretty hit and miss. Etc.

Let's not labour these critiques any longer, except to say that while the best of the books strike me as subtle, careful and reflective about the challenges, few go so far as to express serious doubt about their own answers or spend time steelmanning alternatives. Also, a few are terrible (we've ignored those).

My own biggest doubt is whether the books are ignorant enough (see Chapter 5). That sounds counter-intuitive: smart-thinking... not ignorant enough? How does that even make sense?

Bluntly, more often than we like to think, no matter our data and evidence, no matter our methods or rationality or yearning for an answer, there ain't one, certainly not an easy one or one we'll agree on: not in the numbers and data, not in the evidence, not in the research – which is often less conclusive than claimed – not anywhere.[1] It's a problem sometimes called 'objective ignorance' and it's underrated.[2]

Plus, the more you read (or live), the more complications crowd around even the smart-thinking that does work. Ignore these doubts and qualifications, bet too heavily on answers, models, tools and rules, wherever you find them, and you'll be overconfident. Deliciously, overconfidence is one of the worst vices identified by smart-thinking.[3] And you can see how it could happen and the whole enterprise might backfire. What if encouragement to think more critically has people 'doing their own research', but they do it badly – which, as we've heard, is all too easy – looking for holes in the expert consensus, but going down rabbit holes instead? What if this encourages cynicism about true expertise, deepens polarization, leads to a belief in quack science and conspiracy theories? It shouldn't, and it's not as if we'd want people to be *less* thoughtful, but it's not hard either to see how half-arsed smart-thinking could be a disaster, being what half the loons are doing. Learn to question things, we tell people, and off they go to ask if vapour trails might contain secret vaccines. The simple point is that much as I read it, value it and like it, I'm not sure smart-thinking has been self-critical enough about the limits to how it's applied. Which, if true, would be almost funny.

Midway through writing *Thinking in Pictures* I came across lines I'd scribbled down by Richard McElreath. He's an academic, well known in some geeky circles, less so outside. I realized that I liked what he'd said best of all. Maybe I'll frame it for the gallery, next to the pics.

'It isn't my job to disappoint people,' he wrote, 'but I'm good at it. Other researchers are out there writing books about the wonder of science, capturing the imagination of the public, inspiring the thinkers that will secure our species' just and sustainable future. Meanwhile, I'm telling anyone who will listen that, if we are very careful and try very hard, we might not completely mislead ourselves. There's a chance, is what I'm saying.'[4]

People don't much care for this message, Richard says, a view he attributes to an education in science that 'oversells the wins and hides the losses'. 'It's a form of propaganda that functions to convince us to believe things. But it's shit at teaching us how to discover (or dis-discover) things...'

Does smart-thinking oversell the wins? A big chunk of it, I think so. Some is more balanced, more careful, and there is a handful of books that have come up several times that you can tell I like most, for exactly the reason that they know how thin the ice is. Knowing is *hard* – and if you want only one piece of evidence for that, sample the vast number of medical reversals when the stakes were highest, the brains biggest, and yet what we thought did good still turned out to cause harm, and note that these cases are still coming.

But often we don't want to hear it. We want answers. We love a fix, a hack or a cure-all. And we'd love a reliable method for working out what's truly up; some way of inferring what causes what, and why things are this way, not that – or even what way they are exactly. But the lure of answers is both inspiration and danger. Plus, says Richard, there are many methods for finding answers, and no police: 'Science is anarchy,' he states.

Really? But I think I know what he means. Not that all methods are equal and that truth is a free-for-all or there's no progress. But rather that there's evidence and argument and no choice but to test it hard, use what tips and tricks and expertise we have, reflect, challenge, make judgements, talk about it with others, try again in a state of uncertainty, in whatever way we think best – arguing about that, too – slowly nudging forward, we hope, around and around.

Well, if that's science, what's smart-thinking? The same. Like all thinking, it's vulnerable, competitive, arguable, successful and not, limited and wonderful, sometimes simple, often infernal; we try one thing, maybe it works, maybe it fails, we try another. It's trade-offs and compromises, and often contradictions: we might think privately, but we must argue and often act publicly; we depend on method, but method can be fallible, misapplied and corrupted; to help counteract that, we look to better attitude, but new and improved attitude must be made with the same stuff that drives old attitudes – and anyway are we always sure bad attitudes are that bad? When? Who for?[5]

So smart-thinking has work to do, as I think most smart-thinkers would agree. But it can sometimes read as if the work is already done. That is, it sometimes seems not quite to live up to its own ideals and to become the very complacency it attacks.

But if the books struggle, you're forgiven if you do, too. Don't be too hard on them, or yourself. The ideals are tough, and even smart-thinking will be fallible – why wouldn't it be? This book too will suffer the same faults, and might be repeatedly wrong about the other books and many of its own arguments.

At least, that's my take. But if you take anything from it, it should be not to take even this for granted. There are, as usual, counter-arguments to my cautionary approach to knowing – for example, that there are also great prizes when we get things right; that ideas about which there might seem to be grounds for scepticism will sometimes, despite it all, work like a dream, and all my cavilling and doubting will be misplaced. To decide, maybe you'll have to read the books, after all, and not stop there.

In fact if this book is going to half live up to its ideals, we should, as I've said before, be prepared to doubt this book too, explicitly. So one last mental workout...

Try this

How could the effort to make the issues around smart-thinking more vivid by using pictures be counter-productive? How could the whole premise of this book be misplaced? As many answers as you can think of. Go!

One example: there's an argument from the cognitive psychology of teaching that if we're not careful, what people remember is *not* the principle about counting, which the picture of the sheep in the field was intended to convey, but the actual sheep in a field. The metaphor is more vivid than the general idea and displaces it, so they remember the metaphor, not what it was a metaphor for. Can vivid examples be too vivid and become distracting? Probably. I once heard the story of a teacher who tried to do fractions with a real cake. The kids remembered the cake, couldn't tell you what the lesson had been about. The truth is that I've no idea if pictures help or hinder. I'm guessing, and hoping, and the whole book could be seen as an experiment. Does that appal you? OK, but then imagine another twist: maybe it will so appal you, when you invested so much hope in this book, that you'll now remember to treat all books about thinking with a pinch of scepticism; and since that was the aim, the book will have succeeded brilliantly... by failing. And maybe that will reinforce the ideas about secondary effects and unforeseen consequences, making the whole enterprise a piece of roundabout genius on my part. Still following? Good. Maybe you were smart enough already.

We started by looking for pictures to catch the essence of smart-thinking ideas. But soon we wondered if there was any such thing, and then, paradoxically, we tried to make that our essence, with pictures to show it. Finally we asked if it worked. Suddenly I'm feeling acutely fallible about every step.

Although maybe I'm only big on fallibility because I know, from experience, how fallible I am. In which case, why keep reading my stuff, and why write it? Because there's a chance, is what we're saying. And if we are very careful and try very hard, we might not completely mislead ourselves.

To keep alive the spirit of self-reflection, let's end by wondering by means of a quotation whether by reading this book you simply wasted your time for another reason. But don't simply accept the claim, chew it over. **Think** about it.

Life is not long, and too much of it must not pass in idle deliberation how it shall be spent... to prefer one future mode of life to another, upon just reasons, requires faculties which it has not pleased our Creator to give us.

James Boswell

Read on

2 Unjoin your dots

On cognitive biases: *Thinking Fast and Slow* by Daniel Kahneman; or, if you like it with a literary flourish, *The Art of Thinking Clearly* by Rolf Dobelli; also *The Bias that Divides Us* by Keith Stanovich, about 'myside bias'

One on sexism and racism biases that says they're fixable is *The End of Bias* by Jessica Nordell

A great little read (twenty minutes max.) that makes the case for human rationality and has good links is Tom Stafford's e-book: *For argument's sake: evidence that reason can change minds*; I also like Gerd Gigerenzer's *Rationality for Mortals*, though it's heavier-going

Stuart Ritchie's *Science Fictions* is a great catalogue of bad thinking and bad behaviour in science, and a stark warning to the rest of us

Carol Tavris and Elliot Aronson's *Mistakes Were Made (but Not By Me)* is superb self- awareness-raising

3 Un-count your sheep

The Art of Statistics by David Spiegelhalter is the single best book on how to make sense of data; if it gets a tad mathsy in places and that's a problem, try:

How to Make the World Add Up by Tim Harford

The Tiger That Isn't by Andrew Dilnot and yours truly

Also *Information Generation* by David Hand

On AI etc., two titles that I liked are *You Look Like a Thing and I Love You* by Janelle Shane and *Hello World* by Hannah Fry

4 But count in human

Another on numbers to go with those in the previous chapter: *How to Read Numbers* by David Chivers and Tom Chivers

Others related to risk and forecasting: *Future Babble* by Dan Gardner; *Superforecasting* by Philip Tetlock and Dan Gardner; *Reckoning with Risk* by Gerd Gigerenzer

5 Beware nature's fake news

The Drunkard's Walk: How Randomness Rules our Lives by Leonard Mlodinow

Fooled by Randomness by Nassim Taleb

The Signal and the Noise by Nate Silver

6 But treasure the funnies

The Black Swan by Nassim Taleb: he divides readers; some love him, some... don't, but the ideas are worth the time

The Hidden Half by me

The Improbability Principle by David Hand, about why highly unlikely things keep happening

And for the best account I've found of what's probably missing in the genes-environment model of human development, Kevin Mitchell's *Innate: How the Wiring of Our Brains Shapes Who We Are* is fabulous

7 Focus, but don't

Anthro-Vision by Gillian Tett, who's consistently original and thoughtful

Rebel Ideas, The Power of Diverse Thinking by Matthew Syed

Seeing What Others Don't by Gary Klein

Dark Data: Why What You Don't Know Matters by David Hand

Invisible Women by Caroline Criado Perez

8 Draw the tiger

The Knowledge Illusion by Steve Sloman and Philip Fernbach

The Perils of Perception by Bobby Duffy

Factfulness by Hans Rosling

9 Mind your pictures

The Great Mental Models by Rhiannon Beaubien and Shane Parrish

Super Thinking: Upgrade Your Reasoning and Make Better Decisions with Mental Models by Gabriel Weinberg and Lauren

McCann: a bit 'how to get ahead in business', and there's plenty in here that others would classify as biases and heuristics, but they're right, I think, to say all these are varieties of mental model

Poor Economics by Esther Duflo and Abhijit Banerjee: almost a manifesto for the importance of feathers – for detail and experiment, in contrast to big theory – applied here to developing countries; with Michael Kremer, they won the 2019 Nobel Prize for economics

10 Think bad thoughts

On experiment and its fallibilities, two excellent books on the process of science: *The Matter of Facts* by Gareth Leng and Rhodri Ivor Leng and *Science Fictions* by Stuart Ritchie

And, more positively, David Halpern's *Inside the Nudge Unit*: don't fixate on nudge; experiment to help shape government policy is the big deal here, though even Nudge Unit insiders acknowledge that empirical evidence isn't everything

On policy failure: *The Blunders of Our Governments* by Ivor Crewe and Anthony King

On complexity I'd begin with: *Thinking in Systems* by Donella Meadows

11 Think twice upon a time

For more about being comfortable with an open mind, and especially the emotion of changing it: *The Scout Mindset* by Julia Galef and *Being Wrong* by Katherine Schulz

On being able to rethink and unlearn: *Think Again* by Adam Grant

More challenging on causality, *The Book of Why* by Judea Pearl and Dana Mackenzie makes inflated claims about having solved the problem, but is often brilliant

And *Explaining the Evidence: How the Mind Investigates the World* by David Lagnado uses crime stories to show how we are all casual thinkers who build mental models; this is technical in places

A book on how storytelling works that I enjoyed, and argued with, is Will Storr's *The Science of Storytelling*

Finally, *Everything is Obvious *Once you know the answer* by Duncan Watts is an all-time favourite on our capacity for storytelling after the fact

12 Think in bets

In case it's not obvious, I think *Thinking in Bets* by Annie Duke and *Superforecasting* by Philip Tetlock and Dan Gardner two of the best

I also liked *Ignorance* by Stuart Firestein

And *Little Bets* by Peter Sims

A good, readable intro to the life and thought of Montaigne is *How to Live: A Life of Montaigne* by Sarah Bakewell

A non-technical history of Bayes theorem is *The Theory That Would Not Die* by Sharon Bertsch McGrayne

13 Don't trust

A Question of Trust by Onora O'Neill

And if you're tempted by science methodology, *The Seven Deadly Sins of Psychology* by Chris Chambers works as guide to the merits of open science – a more trustworthy version of normal science – without feeling too much like a formal guidebook

14 Get a new attitude

Another puff for three favourites: *The Scout Mindset* by Julia Galef, *How to Make the World Add Up* by Tim Harford and *How to Think* by Tom Chatfield

The Righteous Mind by Jonathan Haidt

Against Empathy: The Case for Rational Compassion by Paul Bloom

Emotional: The New Thinking About Feelings by Leonard Mlodinow

For a serious delve into the limits of rationality, you could go outside the smart-thinking genre and start with something heavier (but old) like *Solomonic Judgements: Studies in the Limitation of Rationality* by Jon Elster

15 Last thoughts

Final reading: *War and Peace* by Tolstoy, no joke

Notes

1 Why thinking in pictures?

1. There's no standard definition of smart-thinking or its boundaries. In related areas, like critical thinking, the definition is contested to the point where some say it's not even a thing. Does smart-thinking include business books? A few, I guess. Some economics too, I'd say. How about pop science? Usually it *is* pop science, but not all pop science is smart-thinking. Is smart-thinking the same as critical thinking? Not quite, but again there's a big overlap. Same for rationality. There's a border with self-help too, and with statistical literacy, philosophy of science — all sorts. Lacking a clear line, I draw it where I like, without worrying too much, so the selection could well be biased. But I don't think there should be controversy about the qualifications for inclusion of the books I've mentioned here.

2. I should be up front — I've written one or two. But I'm not the only one to wonder what they achieve. Something, probably, is my guess. But there's always been scepticism about smart- or critical thinking, or just plain reason, as we once liked to call thinking well: 'So convenient a thing it is to be a reasonable creature,' wrote Benjamin Franklin long ago, 'since it enables one to find or make a reason for everything one wants to do.' After initial excitement around the new burst of smart-thinking a few years ago, frustration has again crept in. Tyler Cowen, an economist, said of one rational-thinking crowd: 'the notion that this is... the true, objective vantage point, I find highly objectionable'.

3. Jonathan Haidt wrote in *The Atlantic* magazine that the last ten years of American life had been so fractured, so like the Tower of Babel, that they had been uniquely stupid: more outraged, less reflective, driven apart by frivolous arguments on social media. Not sure myself, as I don't know how you'd measure popular stupidity. I suspect there's always been plenty, and I don't know enough history, but, if true, what a turn-up: the age of smart-thinking is the age of stupid.

4. Look up what some call 'the replication crisis' – also known as the 'research credibility crisis' – and the resulting open-science movement. Maybe smart-thinking has helped prompt this reckoning, but I suspect it's been largely peripheral to the soul-searching within the scientific community.

5. Some academics despair of airport-bookstall smart-thinking. Here's Noah Haber: 'the ratio of useful frames of thought to overly convenient stylized bullshit was skewed way further toward the right side than I had previously assumed,' he tweeted beautifully not long ago.

6. In one way, the idea of using pictures felt a bit 'duh', and I wondered why it wasn't already done to death. Maybe it is, just not in a book. Not least, I'd run sessions at the BBC for fifteen years suggesting how young journalists could begin to pick apart evidence, and had always relied on images. Stand in front of a demanding crowd and it helps to have something to show, and the showing seemed to help the thinking. Those courses influenced this book, although only a couple of images made the cut. We took groups of journalists – some new to the BBC, some running small teams in early leadership roles – and tried to disturb their thinking, encourage other ways of looking at evidence. We wanted to make them less comfortable, more restless about what they thought they knew. But we also wanted them to relish the feeling of exploration. So we spent a lot of time going through stories everyone knew to be true that turned out not to be, or where journalists had

put together plausible stories but got the wrong end of the stick: all to persuade them that there might be another way of seeing things, maybe a better way. It's seriously hard to change the way journalists approach stories, especially to stop confirmation bias, but maybe we moved the dial a little. In fifteen years of trying, these sessions were the only element of the BBC journalist training that remained in the course, so either we were getting somewhere or we weren't – if you see what I mean.

7. Graphics can catch ideas brilliantly. Someone ought to write a book called *Thinking in Graphics*. It's not this one. Or, for another way of picturing ideas, read *XKCD*, Randall Monroe's unfailingly brilliant, often hilarious webcomic.

8. David Hume, *A Treatise of Human Nature*, Book 2.

9. Steven Pinker says in *Rationality* that Hume is talking about ends – what we ultimately desire – not the means of attaining them. The ends can be passionate and motivated, he argues, but how we attain them should be governed by reason, and this is the sense in which Hume meant that passionate beliefs, desires and goals are 'served' by reason. The difficulty is when the ends are felt so strongly that they distort the means of understanding. This happens a lot. Sometimes it's fine. Sometimes it isn't. There are also plenty who disagree with Steven that reason and desires, etc., are that easily separated. See *The Entangled Brain: How Perception, Cognition and Emotion Are Woven Together* by Luiz Pessoa.

10. Smart-thinking can give the impression it's obvious that you should just keep your values out of the way when you're trying to work out what's up. Philosophy isn't so sure, arguing vigorously about whether science should strive to uphold a value-free ideal. See, for example, Heather Douglas, *Rejecting the Ideal of Value Free Science*: **joelvelasco.net/teaching/3330/douglas-rejectingvaluefreeideal.pdf**. And Liam Kofi Bright on *Du Bois' Democratic Defence of the Value Free Ideal*: **www.liamkofibright.**

com/uploads/4/8/9/8/48985425/approximating_value_freedom. pdf

11. Gerd Gigerenzer is less of a storyteller than Malcolm Gladwell, and sells fewer books, but he gives a more rigorous account of what are known as fast and frugal heuristics. Try his *Rationality for Mortals*.

12. Dual-process theory says we have two systems. System one is quick and subconscious. System two is slower, reflective and takes more effort.

13. *Don't Trust Your Gut* by Seth Stephens-Davidowitz.

14. www.economist.com/business/2022/08/18/when-to-trust-your-instincts-as-a-manager

15. Though used extensively, dual-process theory has critics. See again the work of Gerd Gigerenzer and others, summarized here: acmelab.yale.edu/sites/default/files/melnikoff_bargh_2018_mythical_number_2_0.pdf. There's even a book on the concept itself, if you're really serious (I haven't read it): *Dual Process Theory 2.0*, edited by Wim De Neys.

16. See Stuart Ritchie's *Science Fictions. Exposing Fraud, Bias, Negligence and Hype in Science.*

17. Anyone who quotes this says it comes from Howard Gardner's *The Mind's New Science* (1985, p.360). But I can't find it there. But Brooks Jackson and Kathleen Hall Jamieson say in their book *UnSpun: Finding Facts in a World of Disinformation* that they asked Daniel Kahneman — Amos Tversky's friend and collaborator — and he said Tversky did often say it and probably came up with it.

18. 'Is AI fuelling a reproducibility crisis in science?', *Nature*, Vol. 608, 11 August 2022.

19. See 'Collective epistemic vice in science: Lessons from the credibility crisis' for the argument that we need a critical mass of 'epistemically virtuous' scientists for the whole system to work. You can't do it on your own; philsci-archive.pitt.edu/21120/1/collective%20epistemic%20vice%20in%20science.pdf

20. See Stuart Ritchie's commentary on 'nudge's travails': stuartritchie.substack.com/p/nudge-meta
21. There's also the sad case of how one of the biggest-selling smart-thinkers came to grief: www.science.org/content/article/fraudulent-data-set-raise-questions-about-superstar-honesty-researcher
22. Daniel is a mightily worthy Nobel winner, but despite the acclaim that *Noise* received elsewhere, I thought it muddled. Though who am I to doubt Daniel Kahneman? Luckily, I wasn't alone. See my review of *Noise* in *Prospect* magazine: www.prospectmagazine.co.uk/arts-and-books/signal-failure-daniel-kahnemans-fascinating-and-flawed-new-book-noise. Or, better, see the review by John Kay for *Business Economics*, which reached a similar conclusion: www.johnkay.com/2022/02/08/review-of-noise-a-flaw-in-human-judgment/. One day I will write a book called *Noise is Beautiful*.
23. 'Cognitive Training: A Field in Search of a Phenomenon' by Fernand Gobet and Giovanni Sala, *Perspectives on Psychological Science*, 2022. See also this assessment of cognitive training, which is not much more encouraging: 'Does Higher Education Teach Students to Think Critically?', from the OECD: www.oecd.org/publications/does-higher-education-teach-students-to-think-critically-cc9fa6aa-en.htm. Plus, link.springer.com/chapter/10.1057/9781137378057_18; and www.ccsenet.org/journal/index.php/hes/article/view/32095; and another in a specific context: www.tandfonline.com/doi/abs/10.1080/03075079.2019.1586330. See also the final chapter of this book on the efficacy of smart-thinking in general.
24. See also *Countering Misinformation: Evidence, Knowledge Gaps, and Implications of Current Interventions* by Jon Roozenbeek et al., which includes a short review of the value or otherwise of critical-thinking interventions.
25. Some technical fixes are fairly dependable. An example would be 'check the absolute risks, not just the relative risks' (look

it up). Simple injunctions like this around common mistakes with numbers do help and are important. But even they can seduce us into thinking that we have a simple answer, and we don't. For example, see Hilda Bastien on the danger of being too obsessed by absolute numbers rather than rates of change, when looking at Covid-19, in her blog, Absolutely Maybe, on the 'weaponization of absolute risk statistics': absolutelymaybe. plos.org/2022/06/02/another-bit-of-pandemic-fallout-the-weaponization-of-absolute-risk-statistics/. Note too that one of the very best numbers-books ever – though maybe I would say this, because it's written by a friend – is David Spiegelhalter's *The Art of Statistics*, and clock that word *Art*.

26. See Stephen Poole's take on the smart-thinking genre in the *Guardian*, 'Can "smart thinking" books really give you the edge?', www.theguardian.com/books/2021/aug/21/can-smart-thinking-books-really-give-you-the-edge

27. By Ben Goldacre.

28. For those who like a formal scheme, you might want to categorize roughly four types of unsettling uncertainty (there are lots of ways of classifying uncertainties, but I quite like this one): 1 state uncertainty (when we can't be sure what's actually out there to begin with); 2 model or definitional uncertainty (when we're not sure we've described or modelled it properly); 3 complexity uncertainty (when we don't know how all the other stuff out there is going to interact if we try to do anything); and 4 result uncertainty (when we're not sure how things will turn out).

29. Though even scepticism has its sceptics. It's too seductive, they say, making you feel clever but never saying yes to anything, so what's the use? Well, maybe, but I think they're confusing it with cynicism. You'd have to be a pretty knuckle-headed sceptic always to say no. Also, saying yes doubtfully is perfectly possible, and sometimes it's the most diffident people on Earth who say it like that – people who don't feel clever at all.

30. Philip Tetlock and Dan Gardner use the dragonfly-eyes

metaphor in *Superforecasting*. It's also almost a rule to quote F. Scott Fitzgerald: 'The test of a first-rate intelligence is the ability to hold two opposed ideas in mind at the same time and still retain the ability to function.' See also Chapter 12 on learning to love uncertainty.

31.   It's worse than that, as the shortness means this book asks you to take a huge amount on trust, since most of the studies that smart-thinking likes to refer to are not included here, for simple reasons of space and tedium. So if you want to check the evidence for smart-thinking ideas yourself, you'll have to read the books after all, and their notes and references.

32.   Astute readers will have realized this is not a work of scholarship or original research, just a journalist with a bit of a background in trying to make sense of evidence offering a few ideas, hoping they might be useful. Edward Tufte talks in *Beautiful Evidence* about 'intense seeing... the wide-eyed observing that generates empirical information'. Good phrase, 'intense seeing'. If any of these pictures or words help with that – grand, especially if it's to reveal the fog.

2 Unjoin your dots

1.   nitter.net/i/status/1471062146100441099. Richard meant use a structure for your thinking instead of relying on cleverness. At one point he says in a research context: 'Avoid being clever at all costs.' That is, do not rely on a flash of insight, but have a reliable, transparent and logical set of procedures that bring us to an answer, and rely on that instead. He's right, of course. See also *The Intelligence Trap: Revolutionize Your Thinking and Make Wiser* Decisions (subtitle in the US: *Why Smart People Make Dumb Mistakes*) by David Robson.

2.   The worst bias? Daniel Kahneman, of *Thinking, Fast and Slow* fame, said it was overconfidence. The rational-thinking royalty guy who said that it was confirmation bias is Scott Alexander,

author of the blogs Slate Star Codex (discontinued) and now Astral Codex Ten, a go-to voice for many who like to feel part of the rationalist community. His blogs are well written, he's curious and very smart, though I don't like everything that's been attributed to him. On confirmation bias or myside bias, the accusation that the other side is rotten has lately gone so far that they're alleged to be 'post-truth', which is clearly meant to be a sort of beyond the pale. But see Keith Stanovich's fascinating *The Bias That Divides Us* for the argument that we are anything but 'post-truth'. He says that when we shout louder at each other about what the truth is, one thing this is not is post-truth.

3. Gerd Gigerenzer, 'The Bias Bias in Behavioral Economics' in the journal *Review of Behavioral Economics*, 2018.

4. T. S. Eliot in 'Shakespeare and the Stoicism of Seneca'.

5. A common definition of knowledge is 'justified, true belief'. Note the 'justified' and then ask yourself: 'how?'

6. Epistemologists also talk about 'reliabilism'.

7. Another, sadder case is John Ionnidis, once a hero to many as a debunker of bad evidence, whose own use of evidence about Covid-19 was – let's put it politely – not convincing. Never have heroes.

8. *Know Thyself: The Science of Self-Awareness* by Stephen Fleming, a great blend of neuroscience and smart-thinking.

9. Hat-tip to Stuart Ritchie, who pointed out these examples. I feel he was a tad hard on them, but the point was a good one: unherd. com/2020/03/dont-trust-the-psychologists-on-coronavirus/

10. Gary Klein, in *Seeing What Others Don't,* dislikes the whole dots metaphor because it suggests the relevant dots are already clear – and what about all the non-dots that get in the way? 'Anyone can join the dots if we remove the non-dots and clarify the ambiguous dots and group the dots that look different but are really the same.'

11. We shouldn't overreact to books about bias as if they doom

human intelligence. They usually say rationality is still possible. The main thing is to think more slowly, more carefully, they say, at least when we can. Though you can't read them without the feeling that humans are ordinarily a bit cognitively crap.

12. Our World in Data: ourworldindata.org/maternal-mortality, maternal mortality ratio 1800–2015.
13. 'Within Reason' at stevenpoole.net

3 Un-count your sheep

1. I've been subsequently told, for example, that farmers count sheep in fives. Is that true?
2. Cassie Kozyrkov, towardsdatascience.com/heres-why-your-efforts-extract-value-from-data-are-going-nowhere-8e4ffacbdbc0
3. A point made in one of the very earliest statistical texts, John Graunt's *Natural and Political Observations Made Upon the Bills of Mortality*. I've seen it said that this was the first such analysis to properly distinguish between words and things counted, by warning that new names of diseases in the bills of mortality did not necessarily mean new diseases.
4. See Andrew Dilnot and MB's *The Tiger That Isn't* for more on this example.
5. See Arvind Narayanan's discussion in 'The limits of the quantitative approach to discrimination', 2022 James Baldwin Lecture, Princeton University.
6. See Dana Mackenzie and Judea Pearl's *The Book of Why*.
7. In 'The limits of the quantitative approach to discrimination', see above.
8. See 'Racial discrimination in mortgage lending has declined sharply in America', www.economist.com/united-states/2022/11/24/racial-discrimination-in-mortgage-lending-has-declined-sharply-in-america
9. A phrase lovingly ripped off from Richard McElreath's blog,

Elements of Evolutionary Anthropology. You will hear it more than once in this book. It's almost its catchphrase.

4 But count in human

1. The UN says fifteen million (www.un.org/en/observances/decade-people-african-descent/slave-trade), Wikipedia quotes twelve million, Britannica says ten to twelve million.

2. Statisticians sometimes get it in the neck for talking as if numbers matter more than people, but most proper statisticians I know are acutely sensitive to what the data mean or represent. It's part of being a good statistician. They remember better than most that statistics about people are about people.

3. After a line from Nate Silver's *The Signal and the Noise*. I also like 'statistics is the art of making judgements veeeeery carefully.' Which is me adapting Cassie Kozyrkov, who's cool.

4. *The Art of Statistics* by David Spiegelhalter.

5. See Tom and David Chivers' book *How to Read Numbers* for some great examples and superb explanations of numbery things like statistical significance. Or try Geckoboard's neat illustrations of data fallacies: www.geckoboard.com/best-practice/statistical-fallacies/, which also includes links to other excellent sources.

6. Inflation at the time of writing was about 9 per cent, using the measure normally reported.

7. Well, it's OK as a metaphor here; later, in another context, we'll get picky about maps.

8. 'Is that a big number?' sounds so trivial it's hard to believe how much mileage you can get from it. But it was core to *More or Less*, the radio show Andrew Dilnot and I started, a big part of our book *The Tiger That Isn't*, and never stops being useful.

9. Teaching journos, I used to put up a few media stories and headlines about risk and then say: 'Right, let's summarize the information here', then scream. Woke them up, anyway. That was about all the stories told to us, I'd say — which was usually

just a scary abstraction like 'risk up 50 per cent!' Reporting risk has improved, but abstract relative risks still appear on their own, and I've seen them from pharma, banks, hospitals, governments, in learned journals – you name it – not only in news or communication, all usually claiming to be big, often not big at all. But see also note 25 (page 303) on the fallibility of some of these otherwise admirable rules.

10. In general, I find the 'number traps for the unwary' type of smart-thinking reliable and useful. Most of it is sceptical, not boosterish, which is as it should be, and tips like 'watch-out for regression to the mean' – look it up – are simple, solid stuff. It's just that numbers about the things we care about most tend to be more complicated than that.

5 Beware nature's fake news

1. Robert Pirsig, *Zen and the Art of Motorcycle Maintenance.*
2. 'Reproducible brain-wide association studies require thousands of individuals', www.nature.com/articles/s41586-022-04492-9; see also 'Can brain scans reveal behaviour? Bombshell study says not yet: Most studies linking features in brain imaging to traits such as cognitive abilities are too small to be reliable, argues a controversial analysis', www.nature.com/articles/d41586-022-00767-3
3. The dog image is often used to illustrate top-down processing, meaning the brain isn't just an image receptor, it uses its own nous to seek out what's recognizable in what it's seeing, and sometimes imposes an image when there's nothing really there. The dog first appeared in an edition of *Life* magazine in 1965, apparently (hat-tip to Anthony Barnhart on Twitter). Its name was Woody. The second pic is from the *Daily Mail*, which called this a one-in-a-million chance, taken by Jarlath Flynn near Gretna, Dumfriesshire, showing a giant hedgehog in the sky, or maybe thousands of starlings swooping for a roosting spot in

front of the moon. Note that every starling is where it is for a reason. Chance, in this case, does not mean without reasons (plural). The chance here is how all those reasons combined on this occasion to look like a hedgehog.

4. You could describe the whole history of science as a slow recognition that what things look like was a more or less sophisticated con: the appearance of fixed time and space to Newton; the solar system as it appeared to Ptolemy; the appearance of design in nature when really it hinges on random mutation and evolution; the endless process of medical revision via theories that we look back on as crackpot. We looked, we explained, then decided we'd been fooled by appearances. Science is forever trying to penetrate nature's layers of fake news.

6 But treasure the funnies

1. 'The most exciting phrase in science is not "eureka!" but "that's funny"...' Also reportedly the words of Alexander Fleming when he was inspecting the Petri dishes that led to his discovery of penicillin.
2. *Innate: How the Wiring of Our Brains Shapes Who We Are*, by Kevin Mitchell, is a superb book offering a plausible explanation, based largely on randomness during construction of the developing brain.
3. The psychology of resistance to inconvenient evidence was the life's work of Leon Festinger (1919–1989), who developed the idea of cognitive dissonance: 'A man with conviction is a hard man to change,' he said. See Carol Tavris and Elliot Aronson's *Mistakes Were Made (but Not by Me)*. But see also Chapter 14.
4. See this simply wonderful paper by George Davey Smith, 'Epidemiology, epigenetics and the "Gloomy Prospect": embracing randomness in population health research and practice': academic.oup.com/ije/article/40/3/537/747708

5. As the science replication business took off, various researchers recalled how they'd struggled to make famous experiments work and had written-off their 'failures' to do so as inexperience, a mistake, etc., finding it hard to believe the reason their replications weren't working was that the original, canonical experiments were unreliable. A lot of funnies were pushed away when, as we now realize, they were telling us something.

6. Note that Marcus argues that shortcuts are not the same as cutting corners. They are, he says, simply efficient. His book can be read as an argument with Daniel Kahneman about whether system 1 (quick) or system 2 (slow) is the best way of thinking. 1 is prone to error and bias, says Daniel. Actually 1 is fine – and faster – if you have the right shortcut, says Marcus.

7. Also suggested by Stanislaw Pstrokonski in a review of the book for his podcast, *Education Bookcast*.

8. The best take-down of *The Black Swan* was Dennis Lindley's review for *Significance* magazine in March 2008, where he said that humdrum old-school statistics was perfectly capable of dealing with the highly improbable events Nassim described. He called *The Black Swan* 'the jaunty pretensions of a literary clown'. Even so, Nassim could still have had a point that low probabilities with potentially big impacts are overlooked.

9. Philip Tetlock has a good go at squaring the circle: www.sciencedirect.com/science/article/abs/pii/S0169207022000371?dgcid=coauthor

7 Focus, but don't

1. See his pages on Flickr: www.flickr.com/photos/thegrizz/6751741963/in/photostream/

2. A line from Dave Dunning, of Dunning–Kruger fame.

3. Various sources and books, including an interview with *Thought Economics*, June 2021.

4. His website is www.chidiebereibe.com
5. In fact, if a patient is worse by the time they're seen, we adjust what we can be expected to achieve and let ourselves off if they have a worse outcome. There's a reason for that: it's so that hospitals don't look bad when they treat riskier patients, but the effect is to disguise the costs of waiting, or at least disguise them from the health service.
6. Also, says Gary Klein, don't only emphasize the negatives. Missing things is the downside. There's an upside from noticing the funnies, which he says is what insight often is, and he has a book about how to gain it, which points out how trivial and easily missed the insights can be: *Seeing What Others Don't: The Remarkable Ways We Gain Insights*.

8 Draw the tiger

1. Hat-tip to Nick Chater, professor of behavioural science at Warwick and a former colleague on the Radio 4 programme *The Human Zoo*, for this lovely example.
2. My view is that we're nowhere near wary enough of complexity, as you can tell. See *The Hidden Half*.
3. Philip has also said that he did not intend to give expertise an all-round kicking.
4. If you're determined, see the paper on Dunning–Kruger by Edward Nuhfer and co., 'Random Number Simulations Reveal How Random Noise Affects the Measurements and Graphical Portrayals of Self-Assessed Competency', written In 2016.

9 Mind your pictures

1. You might not believe this, but I'd written this section, using this picture, *before* coming across Richard McElreath's slightly different use of it in his introductory stats course, *Rethinking Statistics*, where he emphasizes the detailed steps between

circles and owl to reveal the assumptions and connections, and does it far better than I could.

2. My colleague at the Winton Centre, Sander van der Linden, says there are two accounts of how we fall victim to fake news. One is that we can't process it all – we're overwhelmed by the volume of information and it's too exhausting to judge good from bad all the time. That explanation is consistent with this chapter. The second account for our vulnerability to fake news is that we're deeply motivated to prefer stuff we like, even when it's wrong. That's a large part of the subject of Chapter 1. Both accounts seem credible to me.

3. Farnham Street blog, fs.blog/all-models-are-wrong/

4. In *The Great Mental Models* by Shane Parrish and Rhiannon Beaubien.

5. Conflating models with theories will annoy a few people. Strictly speaking, models often include the practical means by which theories apply. I lump them together on the basis that they are all conceptualizations of how the world is, even if at different degrees of remove.

6. There's an overlap here with the dots in Chapter 1. Both the dots and the sketchpad are about how we represent what we think we know. But where we used the dots to talk about self-deception, we're using the sketchpad to talk about trying to capture the essence of what's out there. Different, but clearly related.

7. What is a model? Well now, deep breath. The shortest answer I know is that it's a stylized description of a target system, but after that it gets ve-e-e-ry complicated. There are toy models, exploratory models, data models, minimal models, idealized models, scale models; they can be thought of as fictionalized or as real things in their own right. If you're curious, you'll be well occupied. Look it up.

8. 'All models are wrong but some are useful' is a mandatory quote at this point, from George Box, a statistician.

9. There's a bunch of ways of talking about what I think is the same basic difference, or near enough. Stas Pstrokonski, for example, talks about two 'types of explanation' and offers a whole pile of thought-provoking near-synonyms: Simplifying explanations v. Causal explanations. Morals of stories v. Stories themselves. General laws v. Causal systems. Strategy v. Tactics. Atemporal v. Temporal. Essence v. Origin. Solution v. Process. Cutting the knot v. Untying the knot. Whole v. Parts. 'Abstract' v. 'Concrete'. Art v. Accountancy. Taking the lift v. Walking up the stairs. Market inevitabilities v. Specific catalysts. And, in jargon if you really want it... Nomological v. Materialistic. Try his podcast, which is excellent: **educationbookcast.libsyn.com/50-types-of-explanation**

10. See John Kay's superb essay 'The Map is Not the Territory: An Essay on the State of Economics'. Also 'What's Wrong with Economic Models? A Response to John Kay' by Michael Woodford.

11. See note 10 above.

12. See Wiki's note on Korzybski: **en.wikipedia.org/wiki/Map–territory_relation**

13. *Thinking in Systems* by Donella Meadows.

14. There's a view that a great many of the big breakthroughs in science came when someone hit on a deep simplification – see *Life is Simple*. The book celebrates the principle of Occam's Razor, which suggests that simpler explanations tend to be better, 'all things being equal' – though that last qualifying clause causes big arguments.

15. Mary Midgley, writing about the ideas of John Ziman.

16. Paul Smaldino in *Models Are Stupid, and We Need More of Them*. A great justification of modelling, with a good list of examples that *are* useful.

17. Anne Scheel, 'Why most psychological research findings are not even wrong'. Also see David Hand on 'problem uncertainty', for a technical and difficult but brilliant description of the weaknesses of what he calls classifier technology (the basis of

much AI and machine learning): 'Classifier Technology and the Illusion of Progress', *Statistical Science*, February 2006.

18. In Clive James' *Cultural Amnesia*, borrowing a phrase from Jacob Burckhardt, a cultural historian.

19. See David Hand's paper in note 17 above.

20. I should probably say that the 'outside view' as used in *Superforecasting* refers to underlying base rates for any phenomenon you're trying to predict – i.e. what's the normal likelihood of this kind of thing? The inside view shifts to the detail of the specific case.

21. There's another way to deal with too much detail: forget. The philosopher William James said forgetting was as important as remembering.

22. Wikipedia defines a chair as 'a type of seat. Its primary features are two pieces of a durable material, attached as back and seat to one another at a 90°-or-slightly-greater angle, with usually the four corners of the horizontal seat attached in turn to four legs – or other parts of the seat's underside attached to three legs or to a shaft about which a four-arm turnstile on rollers can turn – strong enough to support the weight of a person who sits on the seat (usually wide and broad enough to hold the lower body from the buttocks almost to the knees) and leans against the vertical back (usually high and wide enough to support the back to the shoulder blades). The legs are typically high enough for the seated person's thighs and knees to form a 90°-or-lesser angle...'

23. Apparently the comment appeared in their book *Computer Simulation of Human Behaviour* in 1971. But I haven't read it.

10   Think bad thoughts

1. According to the Deming.org website – **deming.org/quotes/10091/** – he said this in February 1993 at a Deming Four Day seminar in Phoenix, Arizona.

2. Sidney Dekker, *The Field Guide to Understanding Human Error*.
3. '2021 Suez Canal obstruction', en.wikipedia.org/wiki/2021_ Suez_Canal_obstruction. Was this an example of what's known as tail-end risk – see Nassim *Taleb's* The *Black Swan* – unlikely and hard to foresee, but with severe consequences? Maybe, though small-scale blockages are not so rare.
4. It's interesting to reflect on the politics of what I call kickback, as it could be seen by the political right as a reason for governments not to try to do big things, as they're likely to go wrong. I don't think that follows myself, but it is a good reason for caution. Mind you, the left points to its own list of unintended consequences and other kickbacks as a warning against unregulated private action ever since we overgrazed the commons. So you take your pick.
5. By William Eden, a biotech CEO with a background in rational thinking.
6. 'A Fine is a Price' by Uri Gneezy and Aldo Rustichini, *Journal of Legal Studies*, January 2000.
7. Rube Goldberg was an American cartoonist. A Rube Goldberg machine 'is a chain reaction-type machine or contraption intentionally designed to perform a simple task in an indirect and overly complicated way' (Wikipedia). Whether it's an overly complicated representation of life, I'm not so sure.
8. When I wrote *The Hidden Half*, which is partly about the enigmatic variables that mess things up, someone said, 'Eat your heart out, MB', in connection with this fantastic video of a seventy-trick basketball shot by Creezy in which, amazingly, nothing goes wrong: www.youtube.com/watch?v=Ss-P4qLLUyk. *Touché*.
9. *Evidence-Based Policy: A practical guide to doing it better* by Nancy Cartwright and Jeremy Hardie.
10. Systems thinking as now understood seems to have emerged in the early to mid-twentieth century. There are system-thinking tools, system mapping, critiques of 'mechanistic thinking'

(which is how systems thinking describes the enemy), extensive theory (which spills into complexity theory), etc. My view, for what it's worth, is that it's all fascinating and sometimes superb, but also sometimes tends to overconfidence – though that's what I always say. Maybe I'm overconfident, saying it. A great intro to systems thinking is Donella Meadows, *Thinking in Systems*, quoted in Chapter 9 (note 12).

11. What thought experiments do and how they work (if at all) is another meaty subject. See Barbara Fried, 'What *Does* Matter? The Case for Killing the Trolley Problem (Or Letting it Die)', law.stanford.edu/wp-content/uploads/sites/default/files/publication/259516/doc/slspublic/ssrn-id1781102.pdf. But see also *The Demons of Science* by Friedel Weinart about what thought experiments can, and can't, teach us about the real world. Also check out the list of moral dilemmas, some like the Trolley Problem, that did occur in real life – a set of moral dilemmas based on historical events – from Anita Körner and Roland Deutsch, journals.sagepub.com/doi/10.1177/01461672221103058

12. See, for example, *Poor Economics* by Esther Duflo and Abhijit Banerjee, on the critical importance of what they call the design stage of policy.

13. I enjoyed this interview for the Santa Fe Institute with C. Brandon Ogbunu on the primacy of context in complex systems: www.youtube.com/watch?v=Btrb09E6FF8

14. Bob Hudson, 'Policy failure and the policy-implementation gap'.

15. Lots of A/B testing is apparently done badly, and most of the real results are small beer. I can't follow all the maths, but see *False Discovery in A/B Testing* by Ron Berman and Christophe Van den Bulte, which says a lot (maybe 20–25 per cent) don't replicate because they're false discoveries with, in truth, a null effect. The good news is that they could be done better, but are still unlikely to throw up many amazing results.

16. Wells seems to have imagined a world state, or Utopia, as the summation of all successful experiment. Not sure I'd

recommend *Modern Utopia* overall but, if you're tempted, it's available through Project Gutenberg: www.gutenberg.org/files/6424/6424-h/6424-h.htm

17. See Tal Yarkoni, 'The Generalizability Crisis'.

18. Tomás Lejarraga et al., 'How Experimental Methods Shaped Views on Human Competence and Rationality', www.apa.org/pubs/journals/features/bul-bul0000324.pdf

19. www.nao.org.uk/report/evaluating-government-spending/. See also: www.gov.uk/government/organisations/evaluation-task-force

20. 'An End to Doomerism, Or why I'm coming out as an impatient optimist' by Hannah Ritchie, bigthink.com/progress/pessimism-is-a-barrier-to-progress/

11 Think twice upon a time

1. See, for example, www.theguardian.com/commentisfree/2015/may/12/after-husband-andrew-marr-stroke

2. See, for instance, Hatem A. Wafa et al., 'Long-term trends in incidence and risk factors for ischaemic stroke subtypes: Prospective population study of the South London Stroke Register', *PLoS Medicine*, October 2018: 'Between 2000–2003 and 2012–2015, the age-adjusted incidence of IS [ischaemic stroke] decreased by 43% from 137.3 to 78.4/100,000/year (incidence rate ratio [IRR] 0.57, 95% CI 0.5-0.64)' and 'The incidence of ISs has been declining since 2000 in all age groups.'

3. Gary Klein, *Seeing What Others Don't: The Remarkable Ways We Gain Insights.*

4. Dinosaur idea by Alberto Cairo, the twelve variations by Justin Matejka and George Fitzmaurice, www.autodesk.com/research/publications/same-stats-different-graphs

5. For that sublime visual illustration of how the same evidence can be consistent with different interpretations, see this animation: psych-networks.com/meaning-model-equivalence-

network-models-latent-variables-theoretical-space/model-equivalence/. I first came across it when a tweet directed me to Danny Borsboom's paper, 'The meaning of model equivalence: Network models, latent variables, and the theoretical space in between'.

6. Alex Freeman, my colleague at the Winton Centre, devised Octopus, a research-publishing platform that should change the industry, and she was partly inspired by the dangers of story-making, when researchers reduce complex science to one overly neat narrative. The great strength of Octopus is that it pulls the story apart and lets different researchers in a team publish the separate components of their work.

7. Example adapted from one in the *Journal of Paediatric Research*, 4 June 2018, by Luigi Gagliardi et al.

8. One of the most story-driven smart-thinkers is Malcolm Gladwell; two of the least story-driven are Gerd Gigerenzer and Daniel Kahneman.

9. I've seen this attributed to Arthur Hays Sulzberger, former publisher of *The New York Times*.

10. Another of Edward Tufte's phrases.

11. *The Art of Statistics* by David Spiegelhalter.

12. François Jacob, *The Statue Within: An Autobiography*. Hat-tip to Itai Yanai and Martin Lercher for their article 'Night Science' in *Genome Biology*.

13. See also 'Why good thoughts block better ones: The mechanism of the pernicious Einstellung (set) effect', www.sciencedirect.com/science/article/abs/pii/S0010027708001133

12 Think in bets

1. Not everyone will like calling it that.

2. Steven Pinker, *Rationality: What It Is, Why It Seems Scarce, Why It Matters*.

3. This is the difference between aleatory uncertainty – uncertainty

about the future – and epistemological uncertainty – uncertainty about what we know of present facts.

4. There's a variation on the coin flip in which we know the coin is biased, but not how. Now about the only thing we can say for sure is that the chance of heads is *not* 50:50. Except I'd say it still *is* 50:50, as the odds I give relate to what I know (and I don't know which way the bias goes).

5. Others could reasonably disagree. But that's often kind of the point about Bayesian probabilities.

6. In a tweet by Dan Gardner.

7. Reference is to the *Monty Python* dead-parrot sketch.

8. In a blog for the magazine *Scientific American*: blogs. scientificamerican.com/observations/the-problem-with-failing-to-admit-we-dont-know/

9. Annie Duke, *Thinking in Bets*. 'The discontinuous mind' is a phrase coined by Richard Dawkins for a different purpose, similar idea.

10. One of the most curious thoughts I've come across lately is that a taste for uncertainty might help inoculate us against fake news. See this paper by Eleonore Batteux et al. in the *British Medical Journal*, August 2022: 'Negative consequences of failing to communicate uncertainties during a pandemic: an online randomised controlled trial on COVID-19 vaccines'.

11. Cecile was a professor of epidemiology at Emory University, who also taught about interpreting health stories in the news. She died far too early, in 2022.

13 Don't trust

1. See Laure Wynants et al. in the *British Medical Journal*, www. bmj.com/content/372/bmj.n236

2. A line borrowed from Dan Kahan of Yale University in an interview that I did with him for *Analysis* on Radio 4, though he's used it elsewhere.

3. Another line nicked from Dan Kahan, who's funny as well as smart.
4. I've seen it argued that we can shortcut all this 'who do you trust?' palaver by using prediction markets. Look them up. A prediction market tends to be only about as good as the best expert, but when you're struggling to work out who the best expert is, the prediction market will basically do the job for you and tend to be at least as good as you are at working out which experts to trust. In this way, prediction markets are 'our way out of the crisis of trust' (Scott Alexander again, although Scott himself says that superforecasters are better than prediction markets in some circumstances). My overall judgement? They're fallible, as always, and I would never bet the ranch on them, and they don't cover all questions of expertise, they cover predictions, but they're one more interesting source of information.
5. Onora's talks are fabulous. Pithy, funny, wise. Look her up on YouTube.
6. The Winton Centre for Risk and Evidence Communication, especially its work on communicating uncertainty and trustworthy communication, led by David Spiegelhalter. Conflict of interest declaration: I was on the board until we closed the centre in 2023, as we'd always given ourselves a fixed lifespan.
7. Rules about interpreting statistical significance, for example.
8. Daniel Lakens, an experimental psychologist whose stuff I like and who does great stats courses, once said that being a-priori critical about studies that were hyped was as bad as being gullible about them. You should be neither pro nor anti, he suggested, until you've done the work to understand how good they are. He claims this method gives him a much better hit rate than those who are simply sceptical. The problem is what everyone does who isn't as methodologically capable as Daniel Lakens, when they're faced with multiple sources of evidence. In that case, I say if I've one source that sounds full of hype and

another that respects uncertainty, etc., then I know which I'd be more inclined to favour, at least initially.

9. Note especially that social media amplifies content because it seems exciting, not because it's true. Beware the hot new take.

10. I like Liam Kofi Bright's work on value-free ideals in science. See, for example, his 'Du Bois' Democratic Defence of the Value Free Ideal', February 2017.

14 Get a new attitude

1. *The Scout Mindset*, a good, hopeful and pragmatic book that says we *can* reason our way to better perception, but it helps to have the right attitude.

2. See Philip Ball's fascinating *Curiosity: How Science Became Interested in Everything*. Philip is the real deal in science writing.

3. *Journal of Cell Science,* Vol. 121, Issue 11, June 2008.

4. See Stuart Ritchie's *Science Fictions* for the story of Matti Heino's enquiries into Leo Festinger's celebrated paper.

5. See *Emotional: The New Thinking about Feelings* by Leonard Mlodinow.

6. Jonathan Haidt is a fascinating thinker, but his argument needs an explanation for the presence of truth-seeking attitudes alongside those that are more selfish or feeling-driven, when in so many ways on his account the survival of these better attitudes might seem improbable. Why, for example, has humanity managed to produce a Julia Galef if her ideas are so contrary to human nature? Or is she just deluded in thinking she can make headway against the elephant? Why do some people change their minds, to their own cost? If the elephant problem is that bad, how come we ever accept answers that we don't like? Haidt's response tends to rely on something called group selection, and some critics aren't satisfied by it. They argue that good attitudes are as innate and individual as bad ones; it's all

in there, potentially, in all of us, and his elevation of one side, the side of the elephant, isn't justified, they say.

7.   Cassie Kozyrkov, the Google analytics boss, *expects* it. 'Expert analysts have taught themselves to maintain an impressive blend of intellectual humility, razor-sharp skepticism, and intense curiosity. They're too good at what they do to jump to conclusions.'

8.   'Keep Your Identity Small', February 2009, on **Paulgraham.com**

15 Last thoughts

1.   'The combination of some data and an aching desire for an answer does not ensure that a reasonable answer can be extracted from a given body of data', John Tukey in an article called 'Sunset Salvo' in the journal *The American Statistician*, February 1986.

2.   A couple of favourite examples of things we are surprisingly ignorant about; NB: this is *not* necessarily evidence against either: the value of cycling helmets, **core.ac.uk/download/pdf/13117736. pdf**; and whether breastfeeding really leads to higher IQ, **stuartritchie.substack.com/p/breastfeeding-iq/comments**

3.   Mind you, simply assuming the problem's intractable isn't much good, either, if that view persuades us to give up without even trying.

4.   From his blog, Elements of Evolutionary Anthropology, **elevanth.org/blog/2021/06/15/regression-fire-and-dangerous-things-1-3/**

5.   One academic version of this is that we have to be pragmatic, pluralist (trying different techniques or explanations) and dynamic (ready to adapt). From Sandra Mitchell's book *Unsimple Truths*.

Acknowledgements

There are so many acknowledgements, and the debts are so great, that this will have to be short. I'd like to thank *all* the writers of 'the books', plus all the blogs, papers, presentations, interviews and articles that I've consumed over the years and have now plundered. I'm an addict, often a fan. Sometimes I disagree (inevitably), sometimes I'm mightily impressed. Sometimes I'm there just to see the skill and invention in writing for a general audience, or the determination to get as far we can with a hard problem. On the other hand, if they were up to scratch, I'd be *so-o-o* clever by now... so maybe they're not all that. But more likely it's fearsomely hard to know how to think well, which is why most of this is really dipping a toe into old philosophy. But without them all, I'd have nothing to say. So read on.

Thanks to my agent, Jonathan Pegg, tireless and shrewd as ever, and to Mike Harpley, my former editor at Atlantic, for his faith and encouragement, and to James Nightingale and his team who picked up the baton, again with so much faith in the idea; also to the group of about fifty influencers and commentators that I pay special attention to, who share their thoughts on public platforms where I can read them; and with a big nod to Richard McElreath, who has never heard of me and might feel I've mangled all he said and wrote, but is not least a genius with a metaphor; to friends in this game and well out of it (you all know who you are), and to family (so do you, I hope) for their ideas and love; to colleagues at the wonderful Winton Centre, the RPH and the BBC, for all the stimulation and opportunity to think over the years – to all of you, thank you. The errors are all my own work.

Image Credits

p. 29 The dragonfly view (*Joshua van Kleef, Richard Berry and Gert Stange, 'Directional Selectivity in the Simple Eye of an Insect', Journal of Neuroscience, 12 March 2008*); p. 55 Entrance to the Tin Bigha Corridor (*© Nahid Sultan/Wikimedia Commons/CC BY-SA 4.0*); p. 55 Schematic map of the Cooch Behar enclaves on the border of India and Bangladesh, cropped (*© Jeroen/Wikimedia Commons/CC BY-SA 3.0*); p. 73 Risk, toasted (*David Spiegelhalter*); p. 88 While we're on rock stars... (*BBC News*); p. 93 The good news is (*Richard Gregory, The intelligent eye, McGraw-Hill, New York, 1970*); p. 94 The bad news is (*Jarlath Flynn, Instagram: @photojarjar*); p. 98 Identical, but not (*G. Vogt et al., 'Production of Different Phenotypes from the Same Genotype in the Same Environment by Developmental Variation', Journal of Experimental Biology, vol. 211, 2008*); p. 106 A black swan in a lagoon in Pitt Town, Australia (*JJ Harrison/Wikimedia Commons/CC BY-SA 4.0*); p. 112 Gate without a fence (*pgrizz, https://www.flickr.com/photos/thegrizz*); p. 117 (*ibid*); p. 121 Linda, Volvo's unique pregnant crash test dummy (*© Volvo Cars, Public Affairs, SE-405 31 Gothenburg*); p. 127 Illustration of hypothetical damage pattern on a WWII bomber (*McGeddon/Wikimedia Commons/CC BY-SA 4.0*); p. 137 Draw-a-bicycle (*Rebecca Lawson, 'The Science of*

A Note on the Author

Michael Blastland is a writer and broadcaster. He was the originator, with Andrew Dilnot, and first producer of BBC Radio 4's *More or Less*, Britain's most authoritative guide to numbers and evidence in public argument. He is the bestselling author of *The Tiger That Isn't*, which he co-authored with Andrew Dilnot, and *The Hidden Half*. He also wrote *The Norm Chronicles*, co-authored with Professor David Spiegelhalter.